eapolis
Waupaca Green Bay
Madison Racine Lansing Detroit Buffalo
Stoughton Ann Erie Syracuse Albany Astoria
Lake Geneva Arbor Cleveland New York City
Evanston Toledo Plymouth Allentown
Des Moines Chicago Fort Wayne Columbus Harrisburg Philadelphia
Joliet Kokomo Lima Dayton Wilmington **CONNECTICUT**
St. Joseph Peoria Indianapolis Cincinnati Annapolis Hartford
Springfield Covington Huntington Clarksburg Milford
Kansas City Washington Danbury
Louisville Hampton Norwalk
Conway Pittsboro Norfolk **NEW JERSEY**
Nashville Winston- Bound Brook
Rock Salem Raleigh Paramus
rings Charlotte Camden
Jacksonville Greenville Newark
Pine Bluff Atlanta Edgefield Fair Lawn
Tuscaloosa Columbia Merchantville
Decatur Pennsauken
Jackson North Bergen
Montgomery Voorhees Township

Princeton
Trenton
Baton Rouge
New Orleans Vincentown
on
Orlando Saddle River

Lake Placid
Montpelier Augusta
Manchester
Haverhill
Boston

WHERE THE

SUNDAY

BATTLES ARE

—1953-1959

SPACE-AGE SUNDAY

by Hiley H. Ward

Creative Giving
Space-Age Sunday

SPACE-AGE SUNDAY

by Hiley H. Ward

New York   THE MACMILLAN COMPANY   1960

First Printing

The Macmillan Company, New York
Brett-Macmillan Ltd., Galt, Ontario

Printed in the United States of America

Library of Congress catalog card number: 60-10617

To my three bright, blue-eyed daughters
DIANNE, CAROLEE, MARCELINE
whose tomorrows are in the Space Age

ACKNOWLEDGMENTS

The author is grateful to Dr. Emlyn Davies, minister, Yorkminster Baptist Church, Toronto, Ontario; Attorney Kenneth C. Coffelt, Little Rock, Arkansas; Mayor G. Tapley Taylor, Saddle River, New Jersey; Miss Elma L. Greenwood, associate executive director, Department of the Church and Economic Life, Division of Christian Life and Work, the National Council of Churches, New York City; the Rev. Father Francis K. Drolet, S.J., New York Professional Sodality, New York City; Dr. C. Elvan Olmstead, Elgin, Illinois. These read various segments related to their respective professional fields. Thanks also to DeVere Appleyard, Chicago, who drew the symbols for the end paper map, and Miss Lillian R. Block, who made available the releases and files of Religious News Service.

Most of all, the author is indebted to his wife, Charlotte, who offered many valuable suggestions and who read and typed the manuscript; to Philip Jacobson, director of the Church-State Division, American Jewish Committee; to Dr. E. P. Y. Simpson, professor of church history, Berkeley Baptist Divinity School, Berkeley, California; and to Mrs. Jean B. MacArthur, Elgin, Illinois, all of whom read the manuscript in its entirety and improved the text by suggestions and ideas.

Though these readers helped to forge and polish the manuscript, their views are not necessarily the same as the author's nor does the fact that they so kindly gave their time and criticism mean that they endorse any part of the book in any way.

CONTENTS

CONTENTS

I THE BATTLE FOR SUNDAY

Silently, they sit—the men who fire the rockets.

"Ten, nine, eight, seven, six, five, four, three, two, one, zero . . ."

The landscape erupts. A dull tube pauses, then streaks into the sky. An eery trail marks it clearly. Thirty thousand feet—40,000—50,000 . . .

But something goes wrong. The rocket explodes. For a moment the second and third stages keep on; then all plunge into the sea.

Thus, on August 17, 1958, succumbed the first United States rocket whose destiny was the moon.

When the missile was fired that morning, congregations of Christian faithful across North America were settling down quietly in their places of worship. It was Sunday, the traditional day of rest and worship. These were precepts supported by habit and by law.

Why then the rocket firing on that day?

The pastor of the First Methodist Church, Conyers, Georgia, the Reverend J. Douglas Gibson, along with other clergymen, raised that question. The Reverend Mr. Gibson asked the President and the Secretary of Defense to take a hand in urging "those in charge of research to desist from the use of Sunday as a day to proclaim to the world our greatness."

In response, Roy W. Johnson, who at that time directed the Advanced Research Projects Agency of the Department of Defense, recognized the sanctity of the day. But he said he didn't think the

Lord would frown upon the action. "What we are doing to secure the blessings of our way of life is necessary," he said.

On only four days of the month is the moon close enough to the earth to make rocket attempts possible. "If all conditions are met on a Sunday, we must proceed, asking the Lord's forgiveness for this rude imposition on His day," explained Johnson. He added: "Please try to understand that those of us directly concerned with this undertaking are not God-less men. The more we discover in space, the more certain we are that an Infinite Being exists and is ever-present. I hope that you and others so sincerely concerned will allow us this necessary imposition and continue to support our effort." [1]

The state governments of North and South Carolina were also in hot water for desecrating Sunday in 1959 when the North and South Carolina Southern Baptist conventions protested National Guard drills on Sunday. The commanding officer of the National Guard in North Carolina, State Adjutant General Capus Waynick, explained to the Southern Baptists that such drills are safeguards against a third world war. "We cannot have the proper degree of readiness without some weekend drills," he said. The general explained that Guardsmen on Sunday duty may attend church as a body and that Guard chaplains hold services in the field where the unit is training. "The Puritans," he said, "went to church with blunderbusses on their shoulders."

The mid-twentieth century in the United States is rife with impositions on His day, or rather with battles to set aside Sunday for worship and rest. The Cape Canaveral and National Guard incidents are repeated a thousand times across the United States.

The battleground is more typically that of roadside discount houses, delicatessens, supermarkets, car dealers. The map in the front of the book gives only a hint of the controversies. It cannot be complete or entirely up to date. The author's guess is that there are fifty communities with Sunday problems to every one included. An Illinois community, for example, in which he has recently lived

[1] In a letter to the author in 1959, Johnson said further: "Orders were issued last year to all agencies in charge of the launching of ARPA vehicles to the effect that no space vehicle launchings on Sundays are authorized, except under the most exceptional conditions affecting success."

has waged battles over Sunday parades and the opening of hardware and clothing stores, but these are not indicated. The places on the map are the ones that made the news. They were gleaned from national wire-service reports and from magazines, secular and religious, in the last seven years. Even with this limitation, it is interesting that news stories from forty-seven out of the fifty states received coverage (with Alaska, Nevada, and Wyoming as exceptions). American life is indeed explosive with Sunday-work situations.

Canada, too, is in turmoil over the Sunday-as-sabbath problem. In the last ten years, eighty-two municipalities in Ontario alone have conducted referendums in regard to Sunday sports, with fifty-two voting in favor, thirty against. Nor are the battles over Sunday peculiar to the Western Hemisphere; they also exist in European countries with strong churches, such as England, Belgium, Greece, and France.[2]

Seven Sunday-closing controversies reached the United States Supreme Court between 1953 and 1959.[3] In each case where it has acted (the Crown Kosher case and the Two Guys From Harrison cases were pending at the time of this writing), the Court refused to rule "for want of a substantial Federal question," which is a way of saying that the matter is up to the states. This opinion of the highest Court merely adds to the confusion. It was thought by

[2] In 1958, in England, the Lord's Day Observance Society won its round against the Bishop of Coventry, who tried to inaugurate ballet on Sunday; in Belgium, Sunday newspapers became illegal; in Greece, Sunday markets were banned and churches can no longer be used as polling places on Sunday morning; in France, farmers were rebuked by the Bishop of Parmiers for committing "the grave sin" of working on Sunday. Other Sunday trouble spots on the international scene in 1958–1959 included Hanover, Berlin, Fulda, Eberhardtzell (Germany); Melbourne (Australia); Capetown (South Africa); Barneveld (the Netherlands); Dublin (Irish Free State); Glasgow (Scotland); Belfast (Northern Ireland).

[3] Charlotte, N.C. (movies, 1953); Pine Bluff, Ark. (Berlon S. Taylor, grocer, 1956); Belmar, N.J. (Gundaker Motors, Inc., 1957); Little Rock, Ark. (H. V. Hickinbotham, grocer, 1957); Cincinnati, Ohio (Coleman Ullman, Hamilton, and William Kidd, supermarkets, 1958); Springfield, Mass. (Crown Kosher Supermarket of Massachusetts, Inc., received appeal, 1959); Glen Burnie, Md. (Margaret M. McGowan and eight other employees of the chain store, Two Guys From Harrison, received appeal in 1959). In February, 1960, the appeal of the Two Guys From Harrison store near Allentown, Pa., was also filed in the United States Supreme Court.

observers that the 1958 Ohio supermarket case, which appealed lower-court decisions on the grounds that certain religions were being discriminated against and that the ambiguity of the "works of necessity" clause in the Ohio law failed to satisfy the "due process of law" guarantee of the United States Constitution, would induce the Supreme Court to act. But again the answer was the same: No decision "for want of a substantial Federal question."

On May 19, 1959, for the first time, a United States court acted in favor of a corporation accused of Sunday violations. This startling action came from a 2-1 decision of a special United States District Court panel in Boston, Massachusetts, in favor of a petition by the Crown Kosher Supermarket of Massachusetts, Inc. The branch of the market in Springfield had been ordered by the local police chief to close on Sunday on the grounds that the Jewish supermarket violated the "Lord's Day" statute. However, in an agreement with the plaintiffs, the police refrained from prosecution until after a United States court ruling. Normally, only one judge would sit at the district level, but when the constitutionality of a law is questioned, a panel of three judges is provided for under the rules of the Federal courts. The resulting majority opinion said that the statute deprived the plaintiff of liberty and property by forcing the Jewish kosher meat firm, already closed on the Jewish Sabbath, into a five-day-week competition with other meat markets which are open six days a week. The enforced Sunday closing is also an infringement on the rights of the customer, the court ruled. Since two of the three judges came from the First Circuit Court of Appeals, the ruling had the effect of a decision of that body.

The year 1960 will see the result of this case and others (such as the Maryland and Pennsylvania Two Guys From Harrison cases where convictions were upheld by lower courts). When the United States Supreme Court takes up the Massachusetts case, it may be difficult for the Justices to overlook the ruling of Federal judges that the Sunday laws are a violation of the guarantees of the Constitution. Under American law it is generally conceded that every litigant is entitled to at least one appeal. An appeal from a three-judge Federal court can only be made to the United States Supreme Court. Under the circumstances, it was difficult to conceive that the Supreme Court would refuse to accept jurisdiction in the Crown case, unless, of course, it could find a failure on technical grounds. After considerable delay, the high court agreed on April 25, 1960, to hear the appeal from Massachusetts along with appeals from Maryland and Pennsylvania. For the first time the Supreme Court was prepared to view the blue laws as raising a "substantial Federal question."

All states except seven have some restrictions against Sunday work. The seven exceptions have traces of Sunday-closing laws, but they are so minute that the states might as well have none at all. For example, Nevada prohibits Sunday barbering but is wide open on all other matters; Oregon, having repealed its Sunday law at a general election in 1916, prohibits only barbers and pawnbrokers from operating on Sunday; California has restrictions on boxing exhibitions only; Arizona, Idaho, Montana, and Wyoming also have practically no Sunday restrictions. The District of Columbia merely orders that barbershops and beauty parlors are to be closed one day a week, with the proprietor required to register with the Health Department which day it will be.

Twelve states permit exemptions for Saturday observers: Connecticut, Illinois, Indiana, Iowa, Kentucky, Maine, Massachusetts, Michigan, Ohio, Oklahoma, West Virginia, and Wisconsin. Where state laws do not specifically make exceptions, local ordinances do, as in Arkansas.

Existing state laws provide fines varying from one dollar for the first conviction to possible confiscation of property for the third or later offense. The fines are notoriously low, usually a few dollars. In August, 1959, a Pennsylvania justice of the peace passed out 159 conviction-on-sight notices to violators on one Sunday, and 66 on the next. The 1794 Pennsylvania law called for fines of $4, plus court costs of $9. The justice of the peace is permitted to keep the court fee. Multiplied by $9, he had a possible intake of $1,431 on one afternoon and $594 on the next. In the same month, the Pennsylvania legislature passed an amendment to the 1794 law (which had been reinstated in 1939), approved by Governor David Lawrence, calling for $100 fine for the first violation, $200 or 30 days in jail for the second. (A special three-judge Federal court ruled the law constitutional in December, 1959, with the plaintiff in the test case, Two Guys From Harrison, taking an appeal to

the United States Supreme Court in 1960.) Needless to say, the
Pennsylvania Supreme Court also acted quickly to rule that a justice of the peace can no longer enforce the state ban against Sunday selling without a hearing.

How do communities get involved in these Sunday controversies?
What are the sources of Sunday battles?

RISE OF THE SUNDAY CONFLICTS

A battlefield in the twentieth century is a place of cosmic night-
mare. Everywhere are heard the burps of explosives and the screech
of shrapnel. Blinding flashes search out those in the most protected
foxhole. The scene is a deafening combustion.

So it is with the Sunday-as-sabbath controversies.

The many battles are really areas of continuous combustion.

In any warfare there are the many behind-the-scenes maneuvers,
strategy sessions, and movements of forces. Then there are the economic factors that initiate the war, and the presence of opposing
forces in the same territory.

Behind the scenes, the factors are many. First there is the intro-
duction of the supermarket, the composite highway store, into society.
It is among the heavy artillery assaulting Sunday as sabbath. Such
stores arrive unobtrusively on the heels of a new community. First
one unit goes up, then another, until finally a huge caterpillar-like
store with many segments stretches along the highway.

Consider a middle-sized, Midwest town with a population of
47,000. Ten years ago it was wholly surrounded by corn and oat fields
and pastures. Now there are a dozen new housing areas inhabited
largely by commuters. The largest housing development has 15,000
residents, with the total expected to rise to 40,000 in the next ten
years. Last year a superstore, housing 48 different stores and an ice-
skating rink under one roof, with a parking lot for 4,000 cars, was
erected along the highway bordering the housing developments.

As the young couples move into their new homes, with the sound
of hammers still ringing about them, they are first nourished by the
old metropolis. Then the needs and purchasing power of the new

communities demand indigenous services. The answer is an all-service store, which is all things to the new community.

Now the supermarket or superstore finds it expedient to open on Sunday. One reason is that its chief customer, the commuter, is in the community over the weekend. Thus stores of this roadside type prefer to pay fines for opening on Sunday rather than to close down. This is the case with the Two Guys From Harrison store outside Allentown, Pennsylvania. The 165-year-old Sunday blue law [4] in Pennsylvania until 1959, as we have seen, called for only a four-dollar fine for each violation. For fifty-two weeks in 1958 the district attorney made arrests of Two Guys' employees, but the store, thriving on Sunday business, preferred the fines to closing. One report from this area said that two detectives were on hand as usual to obtain employees' names at the Two Guys store in preparation for making arrests. But the report also mentioned that the detectives mingled with the greatest crowd ever to flock to the store. Now the Two Guys From Harrison stores flank the highways into New York City and elsewhere in the East. Although the chain store is appealing rulings in New Jersey, Maryland, and Pennsylvania, it is questionable whether the new, stiffer Pennsylvania fines of $100 to $200 will stop this organization which does a multimillion-dollar Sunday business.

In areas of extensive employment, especially among new home-owners burdened with staggering long-range mortgages, both the husband and wife work to pay for and to equip their new invest-

[4] The term "blue laws" was originated by a Tory, Samuel Peters, who, after being driven out of New Haven, Conn., in 1781, fled to London. In retaliation, he wrote a satire, *General History of Connecticut*, one chapter of which contained the Sabbath laws of Connecticut as he recalled them. He delineated such absurdities as the regulation "No woman is permitted to kiss her child on Sunday." Sunday defenders today, such as the Lord's Day Alliance, regard Peters' reconstruction of the Connecticut blue laws as fiction; Seventh-day Adventists regard them as the original laws with only slight embellishment, and they cite a report of the American Historical Association which looked into the matter in 1898. The association concluded that more than half of the laws cited by Peters did exist in New Haven and that more than four-fifths existed in one or more of the colonies of New England. Peters, however, did not select the term "blue laws" because of its derisive nature, but because the lawbooks of Connecticut were bound in blue.

ment. In the case of working parents, Saturday afternoon and especially Sunday become excellent days for shopping.

A factor to be considered, along with the superstores, is the automobile. The number of autos on the road has increased at five times the rate of the population increase. The nation's highway arteries throb with heavier and heavier beats. In 1960 the automobile industry "will be lined up in full competition all across the board—from the smallest to the largest cars. For that year, sales records are being predicted with confidence." [5] One satirist predicted in 1958 that the market for new cars will continually be oversaturated, with new slogans developed, such as "Every child needs a new car" and, eventually, "Every dog should have a new car." [6] Already auto sales for the first quarter of 1960 were up 14.4 per cent over the same period in 1959.

The auto takes the city dweller out of his confines on Sunday. Like the tourist who may be passing along the highway on a vacation from a distant part of the country, the Sunday "tourist" from the nearby metropolis finds occasion to make purchases, from meals to cigarettes, from newspapers to milk for the baby. This is especially true where an area with strict Sunday laws borders a lax area. Examples are Evanston, Illinois, where a local ordinance bans Sunday auto sales, and, just to the north, the State of Wisconsin, which in 1959 banned Sunday sales of all autos. The customer escapes south to the city of Chicago with its endless rows of auto lots open on Sunday. The more stringent the enforcement, the more the escape-bound traffic grows. While the highway superstore does not depend directly on people from areas where Sunday laws are backed up by arrests, it nevertheless becomes an oasis for those who flee the city by car.

Sunday shopping is the result of an exploding population. Today there are 2½ billion people in the world; by the year 2000 there will be 7 billion, nearly tripling in forty years the current peak in the world's population. As population increases in the United States, so do the numbers of majority and minority voices. For example, it is possible that the ratio of sports-minded young men will in-

[5] *U.S. News & World Report,* Jan. 23, 1959, p. 40.
[6] Douglass Wallop, *What Has Four Wheels and Flies?* (New York: W. W. Norton and Company, 1958).

crease in the community just as the number of the more church-minded young men increases.

The advertising media dedicated to moving a superabundance of products stirs up the conflicts. T. K. Thompson, of the Joint Department of Stewardship and Benevolence of the National Council of Churches, says: "The new ethic of affluence is a radical departure from traditional Protestant ethics. For this reason it is necessary for the highly organized advertising industry to persuade the average American to give up his Puritan moralism and to enjoy the 'brave new world' which has been given to him by technology and industry." [7] Thrift has been replaced by spending. Buy, buy, buy, "you auto buy now," and so on, are slogans that beat down the will to resist. Selling the affluence of a highly productive society, in a field of keen competition with a wide customer potential, requires another day to do the job. The only course for business is to seek Sunday openings or secure a truce, a course which is difficult but possible.

Many superstores would close on Sunday if they could. Says Herman Gershow, president of Gershows, Dayton, Ohio, "Our policy is not to open on Sunday, but the competition forces us into it." A national grocery chain in Indianapolis agreed to the closing of its sixteen stores on Sunday, and sincerely tried to do so. But in a short while, after a frightening look at receipts, nine of the stores were reopened. In Arkansas, a supermarket owner found that a return to a six-day week cost him 40 per cent of his business.

In many ways various types of isolation cause Sunday friction. New churches, busy with canvassing, organization, and new programs, have very little communion with churches of other denominations. They take their directives from the denomination rather than from a social interaction with other forces of the community. This is noticeable even in the historically autonomous churches, the Baptist and other congregational groups. The accepted theology is that which comes in the Sunday bulletin, the denominational publication, the resolutions of a convention, the decision of a national board. The Sunday idea, in its old dress, accepted by the top leaders is easily transmitted. Members, new or renewed Christians still in need of

[7] "Christian Stewardship and the Hidden Persuaders," *Social Action*, March, 1959, p. 23.

guidance, often lack a sharp edge of decision, not only in their economic and social framework but also in their religious life. Isolation, strangely enough, breeds dogma. An isolated constituency, religious or otherwise, permits supersales programs. There emerges a group response in place of the individualized response that one would expect from a community of isolated units, composed of families, churches, and clubs.

An overemphasis of churches on the family instead of social involvement is a cause for the renewed effort to keep Sunday as a sabbath. (For a discussion of this idea, see the *Christian Century,* "The Second Children's Crusade," Peter Berger, December 2, 1959.) When the Pennsylvania Council of Churches called for a cessation of all "unnecessary" Sunday business on "compelling humanitarian grounds," in April, 1958, its resolution said: "In an industrial and commercial society, it becomes increasingly difficult for families to participate in any endeavors as a unit unless certain days are protected from 'doing things as usual.' " Sunday prohibitions are encouraged where the society seeks to protect isolated units against wider involvement.

The igniting of the Sunday problem is the result of philosophical sparks. American pluralism is guided by practical motives. What works best in the economy, what best serves the greatest majority of interests, is what counts, and apparently this pragmatism is working in favor of the customer, who demands certain products and services for his family on Sunday regardless of what the officials of certain groups say about the way a family day must be preserved.

Skepticism in new formats is also shaping the thinking of American pluralism. "Under the blows of modern skepticism, agreement in general principles, whether moral or philosophical, is a diminishing thing—a serious problem of the church." [8]

Certain brands of Continental philosophy, namely, personalism and existentialism, with their emphasis on subjectivity and crisis experiences, have restored significance to the individual. These intellectual approaches by and large are difficult to reconcile to the traditions of the past. They engender a certain frankness when facing traditions such as inactivity on Sunday.

[8] William Clancy, "Religion as a Source of Tension," in *Religion and the Free Society* (New York: The Fund for the Republic, 1958), p. 26.

Capitalism is not the same as it was a hundred years ago. The dominating minority of the middle class of which Marx and Engels talked is no longer a major feature. There is a dominant middle class, but it comprises the majority of American citizens, from factory workers to executives. The situation has changed:

The interaction between capitalism and democracy is seen to be exceedingly complex and dynamic. The character of both has been, and continues to be, transformed. On the one hand, democracy has ceased to be the method by which different sections of the ruling class, such as the landlords and the industrialists in nineteenth-century Britain, fought out, and compromised over, the question of which should rule, with the, at most, partial and intermittent intervention of the wage earners. It has become, in the advanced, latest-stage capitalisms, method by which, on the one hand, the wage earners as a whole and, on the other, the property owners as a whole, seek to fight out, and to compromise over, the question of which of them shall control the economy. . . . And the transformation of democracy sharply poses the question of which class or . . . which *interest*, is to do the regulating.[9]

Change and greater complexity in class balance challenge the old orders.

The youth, both of today and of tomorrow, are a barometer of Sunday attitudes. While youth cannot be a gauge of the future or of the present, any more than the idealists of the past centuries can, young people at least reflect present-day thinking. When a group of girls at an Eastern college were asked how they would rate each of the Ten Commandments in importance, they ranked the fourth, the one dealing with the Sabbath, as the least important. Such a poll should not be shrugged off by church elders. Perhaps in the more or less irresponsible remarks of youth there is a serious note, a warning.

Greater emphasis on education aggravates the Sunday problem —that is, if a survey of the residents of three Michigan counties by the University of Michigan in Ann Arbor is worth noting. The report showed that greater disapproval of Sunday business was found among "the lower socio-economic class" than among college-trained persons with incomes over $10,000. A similar survey in Minnesota

[9] John Strachey, *Contemporary Capitalism* (New York: Random House, 1956), pp. 344, 345.

in March, 1960, also showed that college-educated residents had less opposition to Sunday business than the less educated. If education relaxes the stringency of attitudes toward Sunday closings, then education expands the scope of the conflicts.

Language changes contribute to the Sunday battle. Most Sunday laws are clothed in archaic verbal garb. Yet states are hesitant to revise the language. For, strangely, when the laws are revised to fit current terminology and practices, they become more difficult. For example, if a new law actually speaks of grocery stores instead of "cook shops and victualing houses," who can say where a grocery store begins and where it ends? The Governor of New Jersey, Robert B. Meyner, indicated to me with a sweeping gesture that certain parts of the store could be roped off to classify the categories of merchandise. Earlier, however, he had tried to face this problem squarely. In a press release of August 4, 1958, he suggested that a New Jersey Sunday closing bill could thus be amended:

Some reasonable flexibility should be provided even when the item is sold as part of a business operation. As we all know, the selling of merchandise is not rigidly confined by category. It is commonplace that a wide variety of small items are made available in the modern drugstore. I doubt that the average citizen would see much sense in a law that allowed the corner drugstore to be open for business on Sunday but in which he could not buy babies' diapers or an alarm clock, but could buy candy or toys. There is a similar problem as to the mechanical merchandise dispensing devices sometimes provided in public places.

Current legislation already in effect or tied up for court rulings indicates that it is much easier to enforce the old laws, applying them where the community feels they should be applied, and forgetting them at certain necessary points. When the old laws are considered for revision, they go out of the door entirely or almost entirely, as in California and Oregon; or if they are rewritten they are challenged by those who are specifically discriminated against. At the time of this writing, with Pennsylvania's amended blue laws in effect, a flood of amendments asking for exceptions for golf, tennis, swimming, picnicking, target shooting, and bowling are being introduced in the Pennsylvania House and Senate. The old laws at least were excusable. People could wink at them, talk of days when

better laws would be written, in the meantime using the old laws
to full advantage to safeguard a tradition. Michigan, for example,
has preferred to keep its 1846 Sunday law on the books rather than
become involved in the consequences of a wholesale revision of it.
Thus the Sunday battles have their inception in the dilemma
which the church faces concerning the old laws. Since it feels by
and large that the traditional Sunday as observed in the United
States should be preserved, the church must, in order to keep the
Sabbath it desires, defend the archaic laws.

Here are some examples of what the church boosters of the blue
laws are defending: A strict enforcement of the laws in Maryland
would forbid grasscutting on Sunday. In Ohio a person cannot go
"ballooning" on Sunday, but nothing is said about travel on the
turnpike. The following two situations actually happened in Canada
in the 1950's, not in colonial New England: A man was hailed into
court in Vancouver and charged with missing church on Sunday;
his excuse was that his wife was sick (see page 97); a Canadian
army captain from another province, visiting in Toronto, was fined
for buying a cigar on Sunday; he chose the jail sentence rather than
fine.[10]

Language-wise, then, the blue laws definitely belong to another
era. But the reasoning of the new laws is more curious than the odd
language. Most current legislation is aimed at grocery stores in one
way or another, and a close runner-up would be the car dealer.
Taverns are often excluded from new attempts at Sunday legislation.
When in 1956 Roman Catholic Jim Moran of Courtesy Motors,
Chicago, was encouraged to close on Sunday, his answer was that
auto sales are just as necessary as sales made in the 8,500 places
licensed in Chicago to sell liquor on Sunday. Moran himself is a
teetotaler. A bill passed by the legislature of Utah in 1959 (but
later vetoed by the governor) prohibited the sale of groceries, clothing, and so on, but said specifically that taverns, restaurants, and

---

[10] Ministers have been caught inadvertently or deliberately in the Sunday
blue-law traps: According to the *Trenton Times*, when the heat was on in the
summer of 1930, netting 3,733 violations in three Sundays, two ministers were
caught violating the law: "The Rev. Don Clyde Kite, pastor of the Central Baptist Church, was detected in the act of buying gasoline, according to police, while
the Rev. I. W. L. Roundtree, of Percy Street, bought a cigar on Sunday" (June
12, 1930).

similar establishments might stay open. On the floor of the Utah Senate, Senator Clyde L. Miller summed up the issue: "Imagine walking into a home on Sunday morning to find the baby crying for a can of baby food and the father saying, 'Shut your mouth and drink your beer!' The bill is just that silly."

Many factors contribute to the flareup of controversies about Sunday. But the new socioeconomic forces are really secondary. It is when these new factors come up against an adversary that the trouble begins. And in the Sunday-closing controversies, these new factors have come up against an unchanging church—a church that is not necessarily rigid in the sense of some of its forebears, the Puritans and others, but rigid in that it clings to an unchanging, unyielding tradition in regard to church habits and polity. Some churches even cling to the archaic ritual in another language, while some merely cling to old ideas. Sunday as sabbath is one of the old traditions, and it has suddenly found itself at the heart of a wide conflict. And while all appearances would indicate that the causative factors are the new socioeconomic forces, the real main factor is the obstacle of an unadaptable church tradition.

Who is really the cause of a war? The nonaggressor or the aggressor? In the case of the Sunday laws, who is to say that tradition is not the major aggressor, if only by the reason that tradition occupies the field, defying challenge? May we not follow the analogy of secular history and assume that the aggressor within a nation is the major party in charge, seeking to subdue its challengers? The situation might change. But at mid-century an ecclesiastical tradition reigns in the field of Sunday conflicts which must ultimately be recognized as one of the chief factors, if not the sole factor, aggravating the Sunday-sabbath conflict.

FOUR BATTLE SCENES

In the Sunday conflict the hero, the church, both causes and commands the battles.

Focus closer upon the battle scenes, to the communities themselves, and see how the battles look. What is the role of the church?

Consider four local conflicts: Saddle River, New Jersey; Little

Rock, Arkansas; Toronto, Canada; and New York City. They fall
into two categories, the secular and the religious.

A sharper examination of the four conflicts suggests a further
division. In the secular category there are two types of situations:
a noncompetitive and a competitive. In the religious category, there
are two: a controversy without a strong minority and one with a
strong minority.

First, consider the two community conflicts which, because of
the lack of strong religious overtones, appear to be secular.

1. *Saddle River, New Jersey: A Noncompetitive Secular Controversy*

To understand the Saddle River situation, it is necessary to view
it in the context of the Sunday-law controversy in New Jersey.

The New Jersey laws, which date back to the English statutes
of 1675, were revised in 1951, striking out many Puritan idiosyn-
crasies, among them a law as to how far a person could travel on
Sunday. The new law ordered closing for all businesses except those
of necessity, but failed in two respects, according to those who
wanted a stronger Sunday measure: It failed to specify the fines and
to specify exactly what were works of necessity. Therefore it was
difficult to enforce. In 1955 a law was passed prohibiting the sale
of old and new cars. Suits contesting the validity of the law were
filed by Gundaker Central Motors, Inc., of Belmar—a concern with
an estimated half-million-dollar Sunday business a year—and two
other car dealers. Gundaker won his case in the Superior Court on
the grounds that the company was being discriminated against because other businesses not constituting a necessity were permitted to
stay open. In the state Supreme Court the decision was overruled.
Chief Justice Arthur T. Vanderbilt, explaining the new decision, said
that the state has power to "enact all manner of laws" in the interest
of the common good. The case then went to the United States Supreme Court, which failed to act on grounds that the case was not
a "substantial Federal question." It left the matter, as it has in all
previous appeals, in the hands of the state.

In Woodbridge, the issue took a peculiar twist. The revision of
the statutes in 1951, after ferreting out obsolete provisions, did not

attempt to make substantial changes. The idea was to leave municipalities with the power to check Sunday activity as each one saw
fit, as long as there was no conflict with state laws (which said that
no place of business, except that of necessity, could stay open and
that, according to the 1955 law, all auto stores had to close). Woodbridge passed an ordinance reiterating the closing of auto lots and
auto-supply places. But the ordinance permitted service stations,
which remained open as places of necessity, to sell auto parts. A
Woodbridge auto dealer took the matter to court, charging discrimination in favor of service stations over against auto-supply
stores. Ultimately the state Supreme Court ruled that this local
ordinance, in permitting certain places to sell auto parts, was flout-
ing the state law, which deemed that autos and auto parts were
unnecessary commodities in regard to Sunday sales.

The majority decision said:

Sunday closing ordinances may not be validly enacted to conflict with a
statute which declares state policy, namely, no worldly employment or
business may be performed, excepting works of necessity and charity
within the statutory contemplation and those activities mentioned in the
statute and placed with the will of the electorate by local referendum
vote. There is no middle ground. The Woodbridge ordinance conflicts with
state policy and it is therefore void and of no effect.

A dissenting opinion argued that what the law was against was
the opening of stores that were unnecessary, and not the mere act
of dispensing auto parts in a legitimate place of Sunday activity,
such as a gasoline station. It interpreted the state law as applying
to a business, not a business activity. For example, Would the owner
of a hardware store officially closed to the public on Sunday be arrested if he entered his store on Sunday to secure a plate of glass
to sell to a neighbor whose window was broken on a frigid day? In
such a case his Sunday transaction becomes a work of charity and
necessity. Nevertheless, the state Supreme Court could not tolerate
a local ordinance that contradicted the general statement of the
state law, and the Woodbridge ordinance was declared invalid.

The legislature set out to try to close the highway supermarkets
and discount houses. With the full support of the Roman Catholic
groups and most of the Protestant organizations, as well as labor

unions and chambers of commerce, a bill was passed in June, 1958, by the Senate and Assembly and delivered to Governor Meyner for signing. However, in the course of being passed, the bill had acquired some highly problematic features, especially in the Senate.

The main difficulty was the fact that the bill excluded counties with a population under 225,000; namely, three coastal counties— Atlantic, Cape May, and Ocean. These counties thrive upon Sunday boardwalk and resort activity. In permitting the bill to get through the Senate, these counties made sure they were exempted. Though noting this major difficulty and nine others, Governor Meyner went ahead and signed the bill, fearing that if he did not, and the bill went through again, it would be sidetracked in the Senate by the three counties responsible for their own exclusion.

Then came the test. Seven large retail outlets challenged the constitutionality of the law, and filed suit. On May 8, 1959, Superior Court Judge Everett M. Scherer ruled the law unconstitutional because it exempted three of the state's twenty-one counties. Within the same month a similar bill had been passed again by the House and Senate. The main amendment was that the law would now apply to all counties, with only those counties exempted which decided differently by referendum before November 15th. On that date twelve counties endorsed the new laws, three rejected it, and six did not include the issue on the ballot. Immediately Superior Court Judge Everett M. Scherer issued a temporary injunction against enforcement of the Sunday-sales ban by the counties endorsing it pending his decision on whether the law was constitutional. Bergen County, in which Saddle River is situated, however, along with Gloucester County, began enforcement immediately. The Bergen County prosecutor persisted in putting the law in effect, thus creating a conflict between himself and the attorney general. Scherer soon ruled that the new law was constitutional, but granted a stay until the state Supreme Court could rule. Within two weeks the state Supreme Court ruled unanimously that the law was constitutional. In the meantime Judge Mendon Morrill, in the United States District Court in Newark, denied applications by two Orthodox Jewish merchants for a restraining order to prevent the enforcement of the Sunday ban. Just before Christmas a statutory Federal court, similar to the special panels recently ruling in Pennsylvania and Massachusetts, upheld the law, refusing to disturb the enforcement of New Jersey's ban. The case marks the first time a local option to enact Sunday laws has ever been contested in a Federal court on constitutional grounds.

In April, 1960, however, the state Supreme Court, in upholding the 1959 law, declared null and void the all-inclusive 1951 measure, which left to municipalities the power to enact their own blue laws along the lines of the three-centuries-old Sunday measure. Chief Justice Joseph Weintraub, citing the First Amendment that says a state "shall make no law respecting an establishment of religion," said the 1951 law went far beyond the point of public health and welfare and had a religious connotation.

The new law says: "On the first day of the week, commonly known and designated as Sunday, it shall be unlawful for any person whether it be at retail, wholesale or by auction, to sell, attempt to sell or offer to sell or to engage in the business of selling, as hereinafter defined, clothing or wearing apparel, building and lumber supply materials, furniture, home or business or office furnishings, household, business or office appliances, except as works of necessity and charity or as isolated transactions not in the usual course of the business of the participants." Definitions, ranging from what constitutes a product, what constitutes a sale and the circumstances of a sale, are predicted to plague the interpretation of this law, as has been the case with the other New Jersey restrictions, previously enacted, and as has been the case in other states, as we have seen, when precise attempts were made to draw the lines between certain products and the modes of selling them.

Saddle River fits into this picture uniquely, for when the State of New Jersey had been unable to give a definitive closing bill back in 1958, Saddle River itself decided to pass an ordinance that would make the general closing law of 1951 effective. It would make the law work there, even if it couldn't be applied elsewhere. The state legislature had been beset by problems posed by competing interests, as well as by state and Federal constitutional questions. There were questions as to what the penalties of the law should be, how to enforce it, to whom it should apply, even if a more inclusive law were passed. Saddle River thought it could avoid the old cries of discrimination and unfairness and "What's necessary anyway?" by closing down everything on Sunday. After all, what really was necessary on Sunday?

At first, when the Saddle River ordinance was introduced on September 7, 1958, it was not intended to exclude the delivery of newspapers and milk. But on the advice of Borough Attorney George F. Losche, so as to assure statutory compliance, the measure was amended to prohibit any exceptions.

This approach to the question sounds almost too idealistic, too impossible for our complex society. But the citizens of Saddle River were prepared to try it. Theirs was a community that was uncomplicated, with only a few little shopping places in town. If the ideal of Sunday closing without discrimination could be made to work, surely it would work there.

When I arrived there on a bright cheery Tuesday in the fall of 1958, I found, not a small, compact community of 1,500, but a vast rolling sweep of magnificent homes, ponds, and swimming pools. Standing in the heart of town I wondered where the town was. But this was Saddle River—the mayor's home was about two miles along asphalt roads that wound up birch-laden hills, and the nearest transportation returning to New York that evening was a mile in the opposite direction at the intersection of a highway and an asphalt road. Thus I soon became aware that I was not in a typical community; but then Saddle River's Sunday problem was not typical either, owing to the extreme and naïve way in which its solution was being attempted.

It did not take long to unearth the ugliness that had gripped the community for over a year, reaching its peak in recent weeks. I was eager to ask the people what they thought of the problem, how it affected them, how it could be solved. The discussion of the Sunday question soon left the sphere of theory. Facts, and the feelings of the people, have a way of changing one's perspective of the case.

A delicatessen owner, in business for seven months, said that he was growing sicker of the situation by the day and that he didn't know how he was going to pay his bills. The passing of a Sunday ordinance itself was not his main complaint—it was the fact that he had come to town and signed a lease without knowing that a

Sunday-closing ordinance would promptly be considered and passed. A delicatessen cannot compete with the supermarkets on a weekday basis only, he explained. It needs to supply people with the little things that a wife, say, may have forgotten to buy at the big store on the previous day. And a delicatessen in any city has to keep long hours, evenings and Sundays. The Sunday ordinance was clearly a near deathblow, a key to the door of bankruptcy, to the little store.

The Strawberry Barn, an ice-cream parlor at the end of a delightful courtyard of curio shops overlooking the lazy Saddle River, also had a story of woe. There was no trace of bitterness on the part of the proprietor, only resolution. The owner told me that he had just broken his lease and that he was getting out of Saddle River by November 15, 1958, which was the earliest possible moment. He had been there a year or so; the Sunday-closing ordinance had proved most injurious to him. Because of the beauty of the surrounding countryside, the presence of good roads, and a massive population within reasonable driving distance, Saddle River had been a tremendous tourist attraction. The Sunday ordinance closing everything had cut traffic to a mere 10 per cent of its usual flow.

The Saddle River city hall was a quiet place, with a janitor sweeping up. A lady was putting some records away. She voiced her opinion: "The people voted for this ordinance, and in order to get the New Jersey state statute to stick we couldn't leave anything open."

"How about the small-store operators who were deceived into coming into Saddle River, signed leases, and then found this ordinance strangling them?" I asked.

"The heck with the delicatessens and the like," she said. "The community can get along without them."

The owner of a hardware concern that had been in the community for years said he had been open on Sunday for two months and was tired of working on Sunday. But he said, "Just because I close doesn't mean another should."

Mrs. Ethel B. Angell, an elderly widow who had been running a candy shop in the community for many years, had her own ideas of Sunday. "I like the freedom of Sundays," she told me. Yes, the

Sunday closing cost her a good bit of business, she said, but she didn't mind losing the Sunday business. Though she had worked for thirty years without a Sunday off, she had considerable sympathy for the local businesses suffering from the ordinance. "They put a good deal of money in their stores, and it's unfortunate to have a bolt like the ordinance come out of a clear sky and chop down a third of their business," she said. "If the town had a saloon, and undesirable people, then the town fathers would have good reason to close them. But the people we have are decent people. They can't be called a menace."

The service-station operators had various views—one had joined with the delicatessen in a protest against the ordinance; at another station, the proprietor said he was glad to close on Sunday; for him it was the dullest day of the week—surprising, considering that he was located at an intersection by which heavy traffic had poured on past Sundays.

My last stop was with Saddle River's mayor, G. Tapley Taylor. A kind, handsome gentleman, with thick white hair, he was confined to crutches, having recently returned home after spending the good part of a year in the hospital. In spite of his illnesses, he was giving the whole question vigorous and honest leadership. It was his belief that if the troublemakers would leave his town alone, the question could be solved peacefully. By "troublemakers" he was referring that day to one citizen who was determined to test the ordinance by insisting that if it were to be literal it should be literal in every respect. As a result of the challenge, the mayor and his council had ordered all local vending machines to be taken indoors on Sundays to prevent business transactions. On the day I was there the "trouble-maker" was insisting that phone calls from booths be prohibited. The newspapers had fun with this one:

You've got to watch your step on Sunday in Saddle River these days. There's no telling when you may find yourself in hot water. You may, for example, chat to your heart's desire at the telephone discreetly concealed in your living room or the back hallway. But you'd better not be caught making a phone call from a public pay booth into which you have previously slipped a coin, thereby entering into a financial transaction with Bell telephone. Of course, you also pay for the phone call you make at home but you do it inoffensively by means of a neat little bill delivered to you at the end of the month, not by crossing the company's palm with silver on the Sabbath.[11]

So you see, the simple situation at Saddle River was not so simple after all. But there were factors that made it simpler than at other trouble spots. For example, commercialism was at a very low level, for the town did not really have a business district and certainly not one that was internally competitive. Second, the problem was aggravated by a traffic situation. The luxurious homes that lined this "sidewalkless" community were adversely affected by the bustling traffic with its accompanying noise and exhaust vapors. Not only were property values affected, but the peace of the community as well. The citizens of Saddle River had a legitimate complaint. Yet property owners in every community sometimes have to face up to reality and change. Saddle River could avoid this reality by directly and completely discouraging Sunday traffic. As far as I could see, the problem was hardly deeper than the traffic situation. The preamble of the "Ordinance Regulating and Controlling Business or Employment on Sunday in the Borough of Saddle River" recognized this.[12] Everybody mentioned it. If this could have been solved, perhaps Saddle River would have tolerated its new stores. For it permitted and encouraged the new businesses. Third, the situation was generally a nonreligious one. This was pointed out by all concerned. No one attributed any part of the local situation to the attitudes of the churches—there are only two: Zion Evangelical Lutheran, which was organized in 1821 and serves as a community church, and St. Gabriel's Roman Catholic Church, organized in 1952. I found the door of the Lutheran church, which was next to the municipal building, locked; I could have arranged an appointment with the minister but I wanted to get the feeling, the pulse of

[11] Editorial from the *Sunday News*, published weekly by the Ridgewood News, Inc., in Ridgewood, serving northwest Bergen County, N.J., issue of Sept. 21, p. 35.

[12] It begins: "Whereas, the Borough of Saddle River is a residential community located in the County of Bergen; and Whereas, due to the fact that the population within the county has greatly increased, there has been an increase in the traffic on the thoroughfares within the Borough; and Whereas, the operation of business on Sunday within the Borough will have the effect of further increasing the traffic . . ."

the community as the situation presented itself through the people. And in this respect the church was not only usually absent from the conversations, but even when it was mentioned it was waved aside as not pertaining to the Sunday-closing issue on grounds that the issue was not a religious one at all.

The significance of the Saddle River controversy lies in the fact that the situation appears to be nonreligious, in addition to the fact that the business arrangement is strikingly noncompetitive and extraordinarily naïve. Yet the problem is certainly not so simple as the town fathers thought when they originally launched the idea of a watertight closing ordinance. As I suggested to the mayor, all that it would take to make the whole issue a religious one would be for an orthodox Jew or a Seventh-day Adventist to buy property and become a part of the town. The ordinance itself recognizes that there is a religious connection, and the rights of a religious minority would receive consideration second to that of the will of the prevailing religious majority.[13] The presence of an active religious minority was not anticipated by the mayor or any of the other citizens, but the possibility poses a threat to the simplicity of this untypical little town. For any little community that can keep out a religious minority or minorities is certainly not typical of the average American community, which leads us again to the speculation whether the religious question can really be avoided. Even at that time a Seventh-day group was bombarding Saddle River with its literature.

All that would really be needed to turn the Saddle River situation into a hot religious controversy, or at least to put overt religious overtones into the whole question, would be for one merchant to settle there who observed the Sabbath. Unless he was examined very carefully, as he set up a business, the Seventh-day observer could change the whole character of this once happy, contented little town, which loves the joy of quiet and peaceful living, by bringing out the religious overtones already inherent in the community.

[13] Says the ordinance: "Whereas, as some particular day must be fixed, the one most naturally selected should be that which is regarded by the greatest number of citizens as appropriate either by virtue of custom or private religious beliefs; . . ."

2. *Little Rock, Arkansas: A Competitive*
Secular Controversy

The Arkansas situation today is much like the New Jersey one in that the old blue laws have been revised. In Arkansas in 1957 the General Assembly passed a law superseding an 1885 statute. The new law was intended to repeal the general statute requiring all retail businesses to shut down on Sunday but to leave unimpaired the right of cities and towns to regulate the closing of businesses on Sunday within their corporate limits. In New Jersey, the state has acted successfully against one business in particular, the auto industry, with a new law now to effect the closing of supermarkets and other roadside stores on Sunday. Also in New Jersey, the problem is in making the local ordinances consistent with recent specific legislative measures. In Arkansas this conflict was removed by the repeal of state-wide restrictions. But in both states, and in all states as far as that matter is concerned, the teeth are in the local ordinances.

I did not get to Little Rock, but through an examination of trial transcripts of the Little Rock situation in the United States Supreme Court in Washington I came to the conclusion that here was not only one of the hottest issues in the country—a perennial problem with a history of severe penalties for certain offenders, but another kind of Sunday controversy.

Basically the Little Rock controversy has two obvious characteristics: First, it is secular in that the people who are fighting the drama appear to be entirely from the ranks of the grocery business. Second, unlike the Saddle River case, with its peculiar absence of businesses within its limits, Little Rock has highly competitive businesses.

In the author's judgment, on the basis of the interest generated, the fact that two separate cases have reached the United States Supreme Court, and the volume of words in news reports, the classic case in Arkansas involves J. H. Hickinbotham and son, H. V., against other competing grocers. The record of arrests for the elder Hickinbotham goes back seven years.

On December 16, 1957, both J. H. and H. V. Hickinbotham

went to jail for inability to pay fines and costs of 43 convictions. When J. H., the elder, became ill in jail, Governor Faubus ordered his release from the remainder of the sixty-day jail term. The son, promising not to operate on Sunday again, was released on Christmas Eve. Yet executive clemency failed to erase $6,000 remaining in fines.

The Little Rock ordinance provides exception for Sunday closing if a grocer observes Saturday conscientiously as his Sabbath. At last count the elder Hickinbotham has decided not to operate on Sundays while his son, who runs a separate store, has elected Saturday as his Sabbath in order to keep his business legally open on Sunday under the city ordinance. He explains that he is conscientiously observing Saturday as his Sabbath, although he declines to specify his faith. Actually, no special faith is required by name in the ordinance. The junior Hickinbotham's battle with the law probably may not be over unless he succeeds in convincing the courts that he is conscientious in his closing.

Two weeks after the younger Hickinbotham's announcement, another grocer, J. W. (Pat) Jones entered the Sunday arena. Accused of violating the local closing ordinance, he was brought into court, then released on a $100 bond. When he was arrested, he said he was a conscientious believer in the observance of Saturday as the Sabbath, but added he was not a Seventh-day Adventist, although the others members of his family belonged to that church. Later, when he testified before the court, he explained that he was studying the faith of the Seventh-day Adventists with a view to joining that church. The charges against Jones were dismissed by Judge Harry C. Robison of the municipal court, who said he believed that Jones, choosing to close on Saturday, was acting "in good faith and conscience," adding that "a man has a right to change religions." (Jones, however, sold his store in 1960, and his successor, Ray S. Cole, was added to the roster of those fined for trying to operate on Sunday.) There are serious implications in the Little Rock cases—not the least of which is the trepidation caused by a civil court entering into judgments concerning the quality of religious faith.

The Hickinbotham case that reached the United States Supreme Court in 1957 is a thoroughly tangled affair. Arguments centered in deciding who had jurisdiction and whether the arrests under the state law now repealed were valid under terms of the local ordinance, and so on. But the main issue is clear: that of competition. H. V. Hickinbotham was charged with creating unfair competition. The nature of the competition is interesting. It is possible that the defense attorney had a point in inverting the competition question, as he probed the matter concerning who was being unfair to whom. Obviously the enforcement was not uniform. Consider this brief excerpt from Pulaski Chancery Court, where the case was tried. Kenneth Coffelt, Hickinbotham's attorney, is examining A. B. Corder, one of the plaintiffs in the case. The Diles store is one mile from the plaintiff, and H. V. Hickinbotham's store is four miles further:

Question—How long has the Diles Store been operating on Sunday?
Answer—I don't know.
Q.—Well it was being operated on Sunday when you filed this lawsuit, against Hickinbotham?
A.—Yes, and he was selling groceries and since that time he has removed his groceries.
Q.—Don't you know he has not removed—don't you know people brought groceries at Diles Store yesterday?
A.—No.
Q.—Would you testify they did not do it?
A.—No, sir.
Q.—Diles Store was operating when you filed this suit against Hickinbotham, wasn't it?
A.—Yes.
Q.—And you knew it was operating, didn't you?
A.—Yes.
Q.—Why didn't you make him a defendant in this case along with Hickinbotham?
Attorney for the Plaintiffs (Eugene R. Warren)—I object.

Later when the witness, Plaintiff A. B. Corder, was recalled for cross-examination by Attorney Coffelt:

Q.—How many grocery concerns, including chain stores aside from the plaintiff's in this case, to your knowledge have contributed to the funds to undertake to get the Court to close Hickinbotham's store on Sunday?
Mr. Warren—I object, your honor.

The Court—Objection sustained.

Mr. Coffelt—Save our exceptions.

Q. (Coffelt)—I will ask you if Kroger Grocery and Black and White did not contribute a substantial amount to try to close Hickinbotham up on Sunday and they are not the plaintiffs in this case.

Mr. Warren—Object your Honor.

The Court—Objection sustained. I don't think that is germane.

Mr. Coffelt—You don't think that has anything to do with it?

The Court—No.

Mr. Coffelt—It shows the interest of the parties. They claim they're being damaged.

. . . .

Q.—If there have been any other persons in the grocery business aside from you who are plaintiffs in this case, that have contributed to your fund for prosecution of this case, do you know what their interest would be?

Mr. Warren—I object your Honor.

The Court—Sustained.

Mr. Coffelt—Save our exceptions.

That is all.

(Witness excused)

Why were stores interested in closing down Hickinbotham five miles away? Were larger stores willing to liquidate him for any reason other than that he was providing unfair competition by staying open seven days? Or were they attempting to create unfair competition in their favor? When the smaller store is closed on Sunday, the shopper is forced to be more thorough in buying during the week, thus throwing more business to the bigger chain stores. As we have seen, the smaller stores depend on Sunday and evening business to survive.

In a truly competitive situation, would not Sunday opening be matched with Sunday opening by the competitor? And if anybody in a competitive situation wanted Sunday closing, would not the request come from individuals outside the competitive business interest, such as a proprietor who is a churchman, the employee or the customer? Competition, with all factors being equal—that is, if the stores were of the same size and type—does not preclude a retardation or cessation of activities. There is more than meets the eye in the competitive Sunday-closing controversies.

Even if bigger stores are trying to create unfair competition in their favor by crippling the smaller stores, one wonders why there is so much fuss about closing on Sunday. If one argues that public welfare and health are the main considerations, one wonders why the rest period should be a certain day.

There is one factor in the Little Rock case that determines that it should be Sunday, and that is found in the official complaint against Hickinbotham itself. The city ordinance is quoted, with its Section 5, which says: "That the City Council hereby finds that many employees and proprietors of grocery stores and/or meat markets are being deprived of the privilege of attending religious services on Sunday by being required to work. . . . Therefore, an emergency is hereby declared to exist, and this ordinance shall be in full force and effect from and after its passage and approval." Among other things, then, a reason for the enactment of the Little Rock ordinance was the belief that employees and proprietors of grocery stores were being deprived of the privilege of attending religious services. Sunday in Little Rock receives a religious sanction from the religious character of the community. Whether other motives—such as big stores seeking more control—help to sustain this attitude is not the main point. A traditional religious rest day is considered necessary and it must be Sunday. These are religious judgments, or if it is insisted that religion does not enter here the judgments are at best secular judgments, ascribing the origin and sanctions of the ideas to religious sources. Which leaves us with a final question: Are such highly involved competitive situations, with the absence of religious protagonists such as the Lord's Day Alliance, church councils, Jews, as plaintiffs or defendants, really secular situations? Or by recognition of the traditional religious morality and religious terminology in the official code of law, are they not, after all is said and done, intrinsically religious?

3. Toronto, Canada: A Religious Issue
Without a Strong Minority

The religious note is obvious in Toronto, Canada, and largely the result of the efforts of the Lord's Day Alliance, with the help of the United Church of Canada and other church groups defending the Puritan tradition. What makes Toronto a special type of controversy is the absence of an effective minority.

The minorities are there. The Jews have a small, new contemporary building in the residential section near the campus of the University of Toronto. But there was nothing in conversation with the newspaper people, the Lord's Day Alliance, or the church groups that indicated the minority voices were sufficiently strong to shape the Toronto situation at the present.

The small Jewish group in Toronto has felt directly an oppressive hand. For example, in September, 1955, when Yom Kippur fell on Monday, the Jewish merchants were forced to close three and one-half days in a row. In that year Saturday was the Jewish Sabbath, Monday was the Day of Atonement, the chief holy day in the Jewish calendar. In between was Sunday, the Christian Lord's day. And on top of everything else, there are city licensing laws which prohibit food stores from being open in the evening. Yom Kippur, a fast day, is preceded by a feast. In a suburb of Toronto one Jewish woman decided to open her bakeshop on Sunday to sell to the orthodox faithful in preparation for the feast normally held that day. But she was promptly arrested for violation of the Lord's Day Act.

In Quebec, where Roman Catholics are dominant and where the provincial legislature passed its own law and dated it just before the time the 1906 Lord's Day Act became effective, the Jews are excused from observing the Sunday laws. Says the Quebec law: "Whosoever conscientiously and habitually observes the seventh day of the week as the Sabbath day and actually abstains from work on that day shall not be punishable for having worked on the first day of the week." Not so in Ontario.

Sunday observance in Ontario is defined officially by a memo issued ten years ago to all Crown prosecutors by the attorney general. It said: "It is extremely important that there should be uniformity throughout the Province in the enforcement of the provisions of the Lord's Day Act." The memo proceeded to outline all the ways in which the Lord's Day Act would apply throughout the province. For example, it would not be applied where perishable goods were involved. However, in 1958, the office of the attorney general agreed to prosecute two cigar stores and a dairy, but no action was taken against a drugstore. This led to some irony in the

Toronto papers, with comments such as "very perishable, those Elvis Presley records, sun-tan lotions, and True Confessions magazines." [14]

In a similar vein merchants prosecuted in suburban North York, in 1958, complained that "if it is illegal to sell cigarets on Sunday in North York, it should be illegal to sell them at the Royal York Hotel" in Toronto.[15]

Nevertheless, the Lord's Day Act is considered a good one by many, for the very reason that it is adaptable. The attorney general is elected to his office; therefore, it is to an attorney general's advantage not to offend the people, or at least any sizable segment of the voting population. For example, in Manitoba where the influence of the church tradition and the power of the Lord's Day Alliance is not so strong, the attorney general does not act decisively on Sunday matters. Even in Toronto, the attorney general's action and enthusiasm wanes, and occasionally reverses itself. For example, recently a directive was sent out to police to make an exception of farmers selling their own produce. "The fruit growers, I suspect, brought terrific pressure," said a Lord's Day Alliance official. "Otherwise why a complete change in less than two weeks?"

Ontario Protestants are in a spot. It is to their advantage to endorse the Lord's Day Act. Fear is rampant that if the Lord's Day Act should be repealed, a law would never again be passed with the same bite. For public feeling is turning against the strict Sunday. The exemplary figure of the Empire, the Duke of Edinburgh himself, for instance, leaving church early to fly to a polo match, does not encourage the propagation of the Protestant Sunday. It is feared that the French Canadian tradition in Quebec, with Sunday wide open to recreation, will take over. Although newspapers are not issued there either, motion-picture theaters are open, not by legal action but by reason of having established themselves without protest in the days when there were very few of them. Sporting events have long been allowed, even with admission charges. With the referendums in Ontario going five to three in favor of Sunday sports, the trend does not smile on the strict observers.

[14] Ronald Haggart, "Ice Box Priority in Sunday Laws," *Globe and Mail* (Toronto, Ont.), Aug. 18, 1958.
[15] *Ibid.*

Says a Toronto churchman: "The Lord's Day concept is in retreat. First it was Sunday tram service, then a number of things like cigaret sales in restaurants; now Sunday sports are getting established across the land, and Sunday concerts will soon be a common thing. In the face of this I advise the Lord's Day Alliance to give up this shadow boxing and retreat; to recognize human needs (it was Jesus who said, 'The sabbath was made for man'), and to come up with proposals for a wholesome and pleasant Sunday. . . . Few Canadians would welcome a commercial Sunday, but most of them would like a Sunday that offered a wide choice of cultural and recreational pursuits." [16] In 1960, however, the Lord's Day Alliance did come out in support of a bill in the Ontario legislature making it legal to hold Sunday "paid attendance, non-profit" concerts, but asked that rock 'n' roll performances be excluded.

The reason for the strength of the Lord's Day Alliance in Canada is that Canada, in some ways, is commercially behind the United States. The things the Lord's Day Alliance was fighting at the turn of the century in the United States—the opening of theaters on Sunday, Sunday editions of newspapers, Sunday sports—are the topics of current battles in Canada.

Sunday newspapers are still virtually nonexistent in Canada,[17] in spite of a renaissance in newspaper publishing and advertising and the fact that Canadian editions of the United States papers from New York, Buffalo, Detroit, and Minneapolis are sold in the drugstores. There is one notable exception—The Victoria, British Columbia, *Colonist.* A morning paper (with 6:00 A.M. distribution directly to subscribers and with no street sales other than news vendors), the *Colonist* is published between 1:30 A.M. and 3:00 A.M. for the coming day. A Sunday edition has come out in this manner for 102 years. But there is never a Monday edition, the editor explains, for

[16] William P. Jenkins, minister of the First Unitarian Congregation of Toronto: "Is the Lord's Day Alliance on the Way Out?" in *Saturday Night,* March 30, 1958.

[17] In the United States, the first Sunday newspaper was the New York *Courier,* March 20, 1825, joined in 1856 by five others. Clergymen found Sunday a good day to issue Sunday-school papers. The last serious attack in the United States against Sunday papers came from Dr. David James Burrell, of the Marble Collegiate Church, New York, around 1890. Rotogravure sections entered in 1910. Today U.S. Sunday newspapers have a 50-million circulation.

this would involve Sunday crews. When in 1957 the Lord's Day Alliance fought vigorously the start of a Sunday edition of the Toronto *Telegram,* the paper could keep its vast investment in operation only four months. Even though the Lord's Day Alliance of Canada considers itself the whipping boy of an ill-humored press, nevertheless, when it speaks and goes to court, it comes out victor, especially in the big issues such as the Sunday *Telegram.* But in spite of its strength, the Lord's Day Alliance is defending a passing morality and is on the way to joining its American counterpart as a loud-speaking little lobby with diminishing returns. When the *Telegram* was charged with violating the Lord's Day Act of 1906, it in turn asked Ontario officials to charge the other two Toronto dailies —the *Globe and Mail* and the *Star*—and a radio and television station with the same violation. The two dailies employ staffs on Sunday to prepare the Monday edition, and the *Globe and Mail* actually sells its Monday edition late Sunday. The Ontario courts ruled that the Canadian Broadcasting Company, along with the three newspapers, had violated the Act and would stand trial. In the meantime, CBC appealed to the Supreme Court of Canada on the grounds that the government-owned station, as an agent of the Crown, could not stand trial. By a vote of 4 to 3, the Supreme Court ruled in 1959 that the CBC cannot be prosecuted under the Lord's Day Act. Both the Ontario attorney general and the Ontario premier predicted that the charges against the newspaper would be dropped also. Said Attorney General Kelso Roberts, "You can guess what will happen now!"

And, as if to show their predictions are going to come true rapidly, the Toronto City Council in March, 1960, voted by 13 to 7 to approve commercial Sunday amateur boxing in the Canadian National Exhibition grounds, ending a two-year campaign by boxing promoters. Prize fights take a legal berth on Sunday now with baseball, bowling, hockey, soccer and cricket.

But whether the newspapers will make another immediate venture into Sunday publishing, even if they could be certain of clear sailing legally, remains to be seen. "It will cost a half-million to launch a successful Sunday edition in Toronto today," the editor of one of the Toronto papers explained to the author. "Who's got that kind of money?" And in the light of the *Telegram's* failure to sustain advertising, who would want to try again immediately?

The Lord's Day Alliance of Canada gets its right to defend the Puritan tradition from several sources. The Lord's Day Alliance was organized by Canadian Presbyterians, and currently some of its officers have top positions in the United Church of Canada, which is an amalgamation of Methodists, Congregationalists, and Presbyterians. The current lieutenant governor of Ontario is a devout Presbyterian elder. (There is one over-all Governor of Canada—now a Catholic, for the first time—and a lieutenant governor for each of the ten provinces.) The rural population of Ontario is predominantly Puritan, and sixty of the ninety seats in the provincial legislature are from the rural areas. Sensitive to the people they represent, the legislators are not apt to let the metropolitan area run away with the Sabbath. Thus the Lord's Day Alliance is a champion of the "defend Sunday" spirit that still reigns in Protestant Ontario.

Things are changing in "Toronto, the good," as the Chamber of Commerce describes it. Sunday is no exception. Nowadays on Sunday when one is in Toronto (a city second only to Los Angeles in total land area), one feels he is on Sunset Boulevard in Los Angeles. Cars zip along the shore drive of Lake Ontario as though in an Indianapolis speed race. The author had been led to expect the streets of Toronto to be like the aisles of a morgue—and they were, early on Sunday morning. But by early afternoon they were like corridors of a beehive. The new condition had been forewarned: "The man who said he 'spent a week in Toronto one Sunday afternoon' drew a lot of knowing chuckles all over the country. Even the natives had to sympathize with anyone trapped in our city on the Sabbath, a fate the locals managed to escape by hopping in their cars and hightailing it out of town. But things have changed. Sunday drivers have discovered Toronto, and gloriously complex traffic jams may soon take the place of the empty streets visitors have found so appalling." [18] These "glorious" traffic jams had already occurred in this Sabbatical city, as far as the author could tell a year and a half later.

The old mentality still has the upper hand, but like all old mentalities, it fades, and though minorities concerning the Sabbath are not yet taken seriously or legally tolerated, a new day is approach-

[18] Toronto *Star,* Jan. 5, 1957.

ing in Toronto. And the more headstrong the traditional forces that charge against the new tide of change, the more swiftly will the Puritanical tenets that the Lord's Day groups stand for be lost. Positive action is desperately needed in Toronto, and there is not a better place for it to begin than in the relationship of a religious majority to a religious minority.

4. New York City: A Religious Issue with a Strong Minority

The minorities are more vocal in New York City, where the Roman Catholic Church is the main spokesman. Chief of the more vocal minority groups are the Jews. The largest concentration of Jews in any one city in the world is in New York City with about 2,000,000 of the 8,000,000 population coming from a Jewish background. According to the Protestant Council of New York City, 22.6 per cent of the city's population has a Protestant background, 48.6 per cent Catholic background, and 26.6 Jewish, or about the same as the Protestants. Of the population, 68 per cent is believed to be church affiliated. Of this number 12.5 per cent are Protestant; 27.1 per cent are Catholic; and 26.5 per cent are Jewish. But the Jews, in spite of their large numbers, are really up against a strong force made up of (1) Protestants and Catholics who have a traditional Sunday in common; (2) labor, which an executive with the Rabbinical Council of America, Inc., believes has a strong affinity with the Roman Catholic Church in New York City; (3) other groups dedicated to defending the majority faith, such as the veteran, patriotic, and church groups. Norman Vincent Peale has said on the subject: "This country's laws reflect the will of the majority, and if we wish to continue living in a land of real freedom, based on law, we must enforce the laws that have been adopted by the will of the people. Sunday was set aside as a day of rest and worship, because all of us need a day of rest and time to praise God for the many blessings He has bestowed on us." [19] The Jews, then, are up against a strong amalgamation.

But the Jews can be a vocal minority. To encourage the passage

[19] "Norman Vincent Peale Answers Your Questions," *Look*, May 28, 1957, p. 66.

of a Home Rule ordinance permitting Seventh-day observers to open
on Sunday if they closed on Saturday, 500 rabbis picketed the city
hall on February 5, 1958. When the City Council showdown came,
the vote was strictly along religious lines, with the Protestant members of the council siding with the Jews. Thus the eleven Jewish
members, joined by the three Protestant members, defeated the
Roman Catholic vote 14 to 7. Three Roman Catholic councilmen
were absent.   1122726

But to be in effect this local or home-rule measure would need
ratification from two-thirds of the state legislature. Introducing the
"fair Sabbath law" for New York City into the state legislature were
Assemblymen Sidney H. Asch of the Bronx and Senator William
Rosenblatt of Brooklyn. There was no question where the Roman
Catholic Church stood. It was unequivocally against the measure.
Protestants became divided. They talked of restudying it. Some
thought that it should be state-wide, if passed at all. Nevertheless,
the Protestant Council of the City of New York and the New York
State Council of Churches spoke out in favor of permitting businesses which are closed on Saturday for religious reasons to stay
open on Sunday. The official statements to this effect were also ac-
companied by denunciations of growing commercialism on Sunday.

On the day of the vote in the City Council in March, 1958, the
executive director of the Protestant Council of the City of New York
suggested further in a telegram to the City Council members that
an alternate solution could be for stores to be closed both Saturdays
and Sundays. The Protestant position, even in regard to the local
and state council of churches, was not entirely clear or enthusiastic,
not to mention the many ramifications of viewpoints in the total
Protestant community.

What happened in the state legislature? The New York *Post* put it
this way:

The Fair Sabbath bill has been defeated in the State Assembly by a vote
of 85 to 61. Having strongly supported the bill, we are naturally disap-
pointed by the outcome. But we are far more disturbed by the nature of
the "debate" which preceded the vote. In fact there was no real debate;
most legislators deemed the subject too delicate for forthright discussion.
Indeed, while 85 votes were cast against the measure, not one man spoke
against it on the floor.

The bill is perfectly simple. Jews whose religious convictions forbid them to work on Saturday would be permitted to open their places of business on Sunday. Under the present law they are in effect being discriminated against for the devoutness of their religious belief.

The restriction is even more grotesque in the light of the loopholes that already exist in the law. The owners of the New York Yankees, for example, do their best business on Sunday without any audible civic protest.

It is no secret that the weight of the Catholic Church was decisive in the legislative showdown. Many Protestant leaders supported revision of the law; some individual Catholics agreed. But leading Catholic spokesmen condemned it, and their view prevailed. . . . In our view the basic issue was equality for people of all faiths. That issue was never squarely met by the legislative opponents of the Fair Sabbath bill; the embarrassed silence was no service to either church or state. Democracy is in bad shape when so many politicians—and so many newspapers—find themselves unwilling to discuss such matters freely.[20]

Why do the New York legislative bodies pay attention to the leading religious voice in regard to Sunday legislation? Is it not simply that this is a religious issue? If the dilemma were secular, such as right-to-work laws, interstate commerce, and so on, then perhaps the voices of traditional religion would not be heeded. But the Sunday issue at hand is a basic, if not the most basic, element in contemporary American Christianity. So it is impossible to discuss the issue in a legislature made up of churchmen, or individuals who respect the voices or the votes of churchmen, without viewing it as a religious issue.

Elsewhere in the United States, as well as in New York City, the loudest spokesman on observing the Christian Sabbath is the Roman Catholic Church. To date, this is not the case in Canada. There, the Catholics, concentrated in Quebec, have carried with them almost directly the gay Sundays of France and the Continent, where once the obligation of the mass is met the day is free for recreational activities such as sports. Canadian Catholics have not been aroused as Catholics have in the United States concerning the "business as usual" trend on Sunday, the reason being, as one Catholic official put it, that an upsurge of commericalism on Sunday has not taken

[20] Editorial, "Democracy and the Sabbath," in the New York *Post,* March 23, 1958.

place in Canada in any degree comparable with the present situation in the United States.

One priest in suburban Toronto saw in Sunday newspaper publishing a good thing. Commenting specifically upon the employment of boys and girls to deliver newspapers on Sunday morning by 8:00 A.M., he noted that the youngsters who got up early had time not only to deliver the papers but could also attend mass. Not so Protestant boys, according to the opposition piloted by the Lord's Day Alliance. The newspaper was not only desecrating the day but leading the boys and girls astray, interfering with their actual or potential participation at the Sunday-school hour. Of course, neither opinion could be substantiated through such a limited publishing venture as the *Telegram* had. Nevertheless the opinions are worth noting. The Protestants, not the Catholics, are the vigorous defenders of the day in Canada; in New York City and the United States it is the Roman Catholic Church.

Originally, the early American colonies were predominantly Puritan. But with the development of more carefully defined democratic procedures through constitutional guarantees and court cases, and through the development of greater sensitivity for minorities by ecumenical and brotherhood movements, the edge of Protestant dogmatism in regard to the strict Sunday observance has been worn off. This defense of the Christian Sabbath has been taken over by the Catholics.

But why is the Roman Catholic Church the chief defender of the traditional Sunday in the United States? I sought an answer from Jesuit Father Francis K. Drolet, whose group, the New York Professional Sodality of Our Lady (a Catholic Action lay group), strongly opposed any relaxation of the present New York State Sunday Observance Law. Father Drolet insisted that the stand of Catholics concerning Sunday was not the outcome of Catholics taking over for the Puritans, but rather represented the spirit of the early Catholic colonies such as New Mexico, El Paso (Texas), Louisiana, Bardstown (Kentucky), Maryland. He explains: "The Roman Catholics in this country or elsewhere are defending the *essential* Christian teachings regarding the Sabbath observance, not a Protestant Puritan tradition which may have *added* certain *accidental* features to Sunday observance. Our concern is with retaining the positive atmosphere of worship and rest and relaxation fitting the Lord's Day."

Many churchmen see a strong stand on Sunday as a defense of the American tradition. Bishop William A. Scully, speaking for 6,000,000 New York State Catholics, calls the "fair Sabbath" bills appearing in the state legislature "completely foreign to traditional American concepts." Nowhere in Canada could the author find response comparable to that in the States concerning Sunday-closing laws and patriotism. Canadians did not speak of Sunday laws as Canadian, as Americans spoke of them as American. But perhaps the association will be made later to serve as a rebuttal of Sunday business activity as commercialism continues to rise in Canada. "Such a statement (that Sunday commercialism is completely foreign to the traditional national concept) would equally apply to Catholic Quebec in Canada should commercialism ever spread there as it has done in this country," an American Catholic official said. Meanwhile, in the States, Sunday laws are decidedly indigenous to the American tradition, according to the Roman Catholic Church and many Protestants.

Observers in New York City had thought that after the defeat of the Asch-Rosenblatt Home Rule bill in the state legislature, the matter would be settled. But scarcely a year later, in January, 1959, a similar bill was introduced in Albany by Assemblyman Samuel Bonom of Brooklyn. In 1960 four more "Fair Sabbath" bills were introduced. Again the bills received token support from the State Council of Churches. But as long as the voice of the Roman Catholic Church is predominant, with concurrence from industry and many Protestant circles recommending or encouraging by silence "good, wholesome Christian legislation" to "reclaim Sunday for the church," as the Lord's Day Alliance general secretary put it in New York in 1959, the preference of a Jewish minority cannot be adequately considered.

One fact emerges from the four trouble spots, from Saddle River's noncompetitive situation to Little Rock's competitive situation, to the stronghold of Puritan-like forces in Toronto and New York City; these are religious issues.

Saddle River will not admit it—but the words are religious, the thoughts religious, with even religious terminology in the ordinances. The Little Rock situation, although not actively involving church- men, has laws clothed in Sabbath terminology, with the local ordi- nance clearly defending workers who want to go to church on Sun- day. The Toronto and New York City situations are obviously re- ligious, with the Lord's Day Alliance as the protagonist in Toronto and the Roman Catholic Church in New York City, both defenders of a Puritan mentality.

When any particular day (be it a Friday of some of the Mus- lims,[21] Saturday of the Jews, or Sunday of the Christians) is set aside for rest and worship, it is a religious institution. When the California Sunday law was held unconstitutional in 1858, Chief Jus- tice Terry said: "The truth is, however much it may be disguised, that this one day of rest is a purely religious idea." [22]

It is true that a government must occasionally rule in matters that are correspondingly religious. For example, blood transfusions, polygamy, the use of peyote (the sacramental Indian drug) are matters of religion that are of concern to the civil authorities. As- suming that these are matters of public welfare, the fact that a government feels it necessary to act in these areas does not mean (1) that laws governing Sunday observances are on a par or of the same order as the welfare legislation, or (2) that when a govern- ment labels an issue that has religious roots as secular or as civil law, that issue becomes exclusively secular. When the United States Supreme Court in 1896 upheld a Georgia statute against the opera- tion of freight trains on Sunday, the Court said: "Opinions may differ, and they really do differ, as to whether abstaining from labor

---

[21] Recently the government of Egypt issued an edict for the National Bank of Egypt to close on Fridays, and remain open on Sundays. Fines are imposed on any who fail to follow "the customs and traditions of the country." Chris- tians on Sunday are given three hours off to attend church services. The act is civil, but the religious constituency of a country determines the necessity and the definition of a day of worship. The Muslims have no real Sabbath or rest day. However, special attention is given to Friday by a sermon added to their prayers, plus a gathering at the central mosque. The reason for the Friday em- phasis, according to Khalil Ahmad Nasir, editor of the *Muslim Sunrise*, is that God created man on the sixth day and honoring God on this day recognizes his crowning achievement as Creator.

[22] Supreme Court of California, April term, 1858, *Ex Parte Newman*, 9 Cali- fornia, 502–518.

on Sunday is a religious duty; but whether it is or not, it is certain that the legislature of Georgia has prescribed it as a civil duty." [23] In explaining the new 1959 Pennsylvania amendment, Circuit Judge William Hastie, who wrote the majority opinion in the Federal decision upholding the law, said: "We find nothing in the case discussing the Pennsylvania legislation and its background which makes any plainer the religious considerations which underlie the adoption of the 'Blue Laws' of that state and from time to time have been utilized to justify them. The historical religious connection is so clear as to be obvious and indisputable. It has been stressed that the Supreme Court of Pennsylvania in upholding the local statute has gone so far as to say that 'Christianity is part of the common law of Pennsylvania.'"

The intent of any law can be interpreted in many ways. The Sunday laws are no exception. Religious voices will continue to defend them as being necessary rest laws. But no matter how Sunday laws are regarded, the fact remains, as even the courts insist when recognizing the Sunday laws as part of common law, that they are religious laws.

[23] Hennington versus Georgia, 163 U.S. 299, 307.

II REST IN THE SPACE AGE

Already Sunday is in jeopardy. The many challenges to Sunday laws, as we have seen, make this clear. Whether Sunday is a passing tradition or not, certain aspects of Sunday are passing. Missile firings, sport events, taverns, supermarkets, auto stores, model homes, theaters, newspapers—all indicate a heavy amount of activity on Sunday unrelated to the traditional Sunday habits of worship and works of charity. Sunday is losing its luster, its historical reputation as a memorial to Christ's resurrection, and as a quasi-Jewish rest day.

Now all this is alarming to the layman, as well as to the clergyman. The layman does not really mind seeing Sunday going—he has no real attachment spiritually to the day. But he does expect the day. It is a part of his schedule. If the grip which the church has on the state in regard to its holy day is relaxed, then will he really have a day at all to do what he wants—whether it be to worship or to engage in recreation?

If there were no major force pressuring to keep Sunday as a rest day or holiday, what would happen to the day? State officials have no real taste for the day other than that of pleasing a constituency. Governor George D. Clyde of Utah in vetoing a general Sunday closing law in 1959 said it would work hardships on the economy and reduce tax revenue as the mines and factories were shut down. Unions, which no longer speak out for Sunday per se on a national level,[1] hold meetings on Sunday in Oregon commu-

[1] Says Tilford E. Dudley, director of the Speakers Bureau of the AFL-CIO:

nities and other states. Without the church batting for him and
without the state enforcing his "religious" views as supplied by the
church and church history, the average man would really be in
trouble.

Who wants to work seven days a week? That this will happen if
business and other interests get our Sunday is common parlance.
There is quickly conjured up the anonymous state of a classless or
feudal society, such as modern China, in which everybody works
seven days a week from early morning to sunset.[2] This is terribly
frightening to a nation that is accustomed to some leisure time,
especially on a regular weekly basis. If we work every day, we shall
become no better than a slave society; it is argued that, instead of
being slave to a production quota in a Communist nation, we will
in fact be slave to a production quota in the United States.

It is hard to think of losing Sunday—especially for the layman,
and especially if he does not go to church. A strange thought, is it
not? The nonchurchgoer needs this church day more than the con-
secrated Christian. His philosophy dictates it or feeds upon it, his
philosophy of noninvolvement, of living a humdrum existence. An
advertising man was telling me recently that when he flew to New
York from Chicago on business, if the business should carry over to
Monday the company always flew him home for the weekend and
then back on Monday. The day was that important.

The Christian can get along without Sunday. If worship has to
be on one day, he can usually take in earlier services, especially if

---

"A resolution on Sunday work was prepared for our merger convention held in
New York in December, 1955. It was one of those that did not get to the floor
and was referred to the Executive Council for Action. However, the Executive
Council took no action and left the matter to the various International Unions
for handling in the formulation of their policies for their negotiations with em-
ployers concerning hours of work, over-time, etc." Formerly labor leaders and
unions spoke out jointly with the earlier American Sabbath Union. But now
longer work hours are not feared; in fact, many unions welcome the opportunity
to work overtime on account of time-and-a-half pay or double pay on Sundays.

[2] Cf. "Red China Bid for a Future: The Great Leap Forward," *Life*, Jan. 5,
1959, pp. 45–66: "On the island of Lappa . . . China's Communist masters
have established . . . a people's Commune. The daily toil . . . lasts from 5 A.M.
till midnight when the last platoon of weary workers stumbles back to the bar-
racks . . . 19 hours a day, 7 days a week it goes on. . . . The routine was the
same, day in, day out, 7 days a week. The only days off were national holidays."

he lives in a big city or is a Roman Catholic, and then work the rest of the day. Worship is no problem. And neither is the rest situation. He can get along without a traditional day of rest. This does not mean to say that he does not need rest. But his life is more readily adapted to another schedule. And the reason is that he makes a distinction between the different kinds of rest.

To the Christian there are two kinds of rest, physical and spiritual. The church has confused the two at times, Sunday being regarded as a day of physical rest. The line of demarcation between the two is clear to the Christian but blurred to the layman.

What are the recommendations of a secular approach to rest for the Space Age, what are the recommendations of a spiritual approach to the same subject, and finally what is the total impact on a Sunday idea when all current ideas are synthesized and considered by the Christian who has a foot in both a city of God and a city of the earth?

First, what is the trend in secular ideas of physical or bodily rest in the Space Age?

These points come to the fore:

1. *Rest is relative.* In regard to sleeping, two people do not need the same amount of sleep. Says Dr. Joe Kamiya, director, Dream and Sleep Research Project, University of Chicago: "Among adults there are those who require 9 hours or even 10 every night, and those who do perfectly well on 5 or 6. There's no magic to the number 8 as far as hours of sleep are concerned. Knowing the average—which happens to be about 7.5 hours—doesn't help you at all. I'm sure you wouldn't buy a pair of shoes just because they were of average size." [3] Also, a person varies in his needs relative to his other tasks. For example, Edison and Napoleon slept only four hours a night and catnapped during the day. Some jobs demand more rest—a person working night and day needs one or two days off for sleep while a man with a regular schedule might need a set seven or eight hours a night. The same holds for recreation and diversions. People's needs and habits vary.

2. *Work can be rest.* Ever get stuck in a small town with nothing to do, with plenty of opportunity to rest, but that is all? Now, if

[3] "How Much Sleep Do You Really Need?" *U.S. News & World Report,* Feb. 6, 1959, p. 68.

you were stranded in the same town with your auto, and you had a chance to wash it or write letters or even dig a ditch, would you enjoy this more than just sitting around? This point has been recognized more recently in regard to therapy in state institutions, in care of the infirm and aged—give them something to do. Thus in some communities for old folks, such as the Methodist old folks' home in Selma, Alabama, the old folks are housed in a village-like arrangement with all the responsibilities of a city. In penology, work farms have proved more rehabilitative than inactivity in a cell. Your own workaday job also can provide more rest than a Sunday of inactivity. Said Arthur Little, quoted in the *Watchman-Examiner:* "Nothing is so wholesome and medicinal for an aching heart as work, continuous employment. Sorrow is apt to be introspective, self-centered and, in the estimate of the sufferer, exceptional. Isolation and solitude are too often thought to be its congenial employment; whereas open air, sunshine and a busy life are a sovereign balm for the saddest soul." [4] Life is so short, a "vapor," as the Epistle of James puts it, that a person needs to rest within his vocation. Says Camus, describing an artist gradually going mad trying to hit a happy balance between work and play: "But life is short, time races by, and his own energy had limits. It was hard to paint the world and men and, at the same time, to live with them." [5] Sometimes rest must be sought in work.

3. *Tension, not a tranquilizer, can be restful.* It depends on what the tension is.

Most of us have failed to realize that tension is desirable—that without it we would get as much pleasure out of life as a jellyfish. Without tension, man cannot operate. Dr. M. Nyswander, a diplomate of the American Board of Psychiatry and Neurology, says bluntly, "I cannot be too emphatic about the desirability of tension." And new investigations in industry tend to support the doctor's viewpoint. . . . Willingness to accept tension and use it effectively is often the key to enjoyment of life. . . . Dr. Dana L. Farnsworth, professor of hygiene and director of university health services at Harvard University, has stated: "Conformity, constant happi-

---

[4] Jan. 12, 1959, p. 57.
[5] Albert Camus, *Exile and the Kingdom,* translated by Justin O'Brien, "The Artist at Work" (New York: Alfred A. Knopf, 1958), p. 135.

ness, and absence of stress and anxiety are not reasonable goals in a democracy. Conflict is an inescapable part of modern living, and the resolution of conflicts produces real satisfaction." [6]

As Harold Blake Walker, minister of First Presbyterian Church, Evanston, Illinois, points out: "It is not our work that wears us down. It is our waste of energy in worry, fear, and hate." [7]

4. *No absolute principle governs rest.* "No one possesses the one truth for all." [8] What is valid for one person is not necessarily valid for another. Likewise, what was valid under a theocracy in the past, with certain conditions of labor, is not necessarily valid under a democratic form of government with radically different labor arrangements. "When a man was supposed to work so hard during the week that he was completely exhausted by Sunday, a day of rest was an absolute necessity. Nowadays with the 40-hour week generally in effect the exhaustion has disappeared and on Sunday the average citizen is ready for some recreation. . . ." [9]

5. *Patterns of rest vary.* While the state has the right to protect the health of its people, in so doing it must recognize that rest patterns have changed and are changing. Automation, unemployment, labor bargaining—all have led us to think in terms of longer weekends instead of Sunday leisure time. When I was talking with a friend recently about some of the recommendations of this book, he reiterated his dependency on Sunday as a day of refreshment from his busy schedule. In defending his Sunday rest, he said: "I don't know what I'd do without my weekends." His own words summed up the whole matter. He was no longer really thinking in terms of Sunday, but rather in terms of a weekend.

In fact, if the churches insist on joining forces with labor to secure adequate rest for man (as they joined to achieve a Sabbath's rest at the turn of the century), then the church must talk in terms of weekends and evenings. The AFL-CIO resolutions in 1959 asked for a

[6] E. M. D. Watson, "Thriving on Tension," *Cosmopolitan,* February, 1958.
[7] Chicago *Sunday Tribune Magazine,* "Hurry and Worry, Not Work, Are Our Enemies," Oct. 11, 1959, p. 52.
[8] Karl Jaspers in *Myth and Christianity,* by Karl Jaspers and Rudolf Bultmann (New York: The Noonday Press, 1958), p. 82.
[9] J. V. McAree, "Sunday Blue Laws," *Toronto Globe and Mail,* Dec. 3, 1956.

revision of the Fair Labor Standards Act to provide for a 7-hour day, 35-hour week instead of the 40-hour week established twenty years ago. A one-day's rest is a lost term in labor's vocabulary today.

6. *Vocation can determine the kind of rest.* "The nature of our leisure will be governed by our work," said a report at the Conference on Christian Politics, Economics and Citizenship in Birmingham,[10] back in 1924. If a person likes his work, chances are he will have no desire to divorce it entirely from his free time. That is not to say that the white-collar worker would want to carry armfuls of work home with him, or the factory worker his machine. But his vocational interest cannot really check out with him when he punches the time clock. Work is like other relationships. A person does not carry his wife and family with him to work, but he might carry some remembrance of them, a picture on his desk or in his billfold. Life is not segregated. Thus, as an editor and reporter, I am quite happy at home, after the kids have gone to bed, spending a few hours pounding out a free-lance piece. Cleaning out furnaces, putting up storm windows or taking them down and trading them for screens, washing the car, painting the house do not really charm me, although they are relaxing—in their way. I prefer to feed my typewriter, whose appetite has become atrocious. I have a brother-in-law who is an expert Diesel mechanic and spends long hours on the job; yet he loves to spend evenings and weekends tinkering with cars. What we do in our leisure time can be closely related to what we do as a vocation during the week.

7. *Rest should be meaningful.* Even without definite religious overtones, rest should be meaningful. Otherwise it is mere boredom; a person does it because the holiday comes along, or because he has to. There should be conscious decision, some purpose, some intent, some goals. Automation threatens the elimination of meaning in rest and leisure, for it comes so quickly, with the community, the employer, or work force usually uninformed as to what to do. Robert Hutchins warns against the lack of preparation for this new leisure. A "great problem of the future for man may be what to do with himself when he works only 20 hours a week. Suicidal tendencies are associated with boredom, and leisure may destroy man unless

[10] Published by Longmans, Green and Company, New York, 1924, p. 6.

education teaches him how to utilize it intelligently." [11] Rest, as leisure time, should be meaningful, otherwise one would be better without it. The problem of leisure was so pressing in the 1959 British elections that the Conservatives called their program "Challenge of Leisure," while Labor's proposals were "Leisure of Living."

Rest, then, in the physical sense is not so simple as we normally suppose. It is not as simple as the Lord's Day people make it out to be. The statement is not true that "the rhythm of life demands a weekly day for rest and worship, free from noise and excitement." [12] Physiologically, psychologically, sociologically, a person may need just the opposite of what his brother needs. The legislature cannot tell him as precisely as we want him told. We cannot say in a modern age that a person needs one day a week of rest, much less a certain kind of rest on a certain kind of day.

Now spiritual rest, provided in the Christian faith, does touch certain areas of a person's physical or psychological rest, such as his need for meaning in what he does. But spiritual rest is not measurable by objective standards. It has in it an element of eschatology not understood by secular criteria, although the effect of living in relationship with a living Christ on the way a person acts may show that he is satisfied, that he has found a certain rest or peace of mind.

What is spiritual rest like, the rest that Christ gives? In the first place, it is not quantitative, nor is it derived from a quantitative arrangement in space or time. There are many words translated "rest" in the Bible, some of which could be better translated into other words, such as "silence" or "quiet" for "rest" in Isaiah 62:7 (Hebrew: *domi*); "cessation" or "rest"—the literal translation of "sabbath"; or "peace," as in Acts 9:31—"Then had the churches rest [*eirene*, or "peace"] throughout all Judæa. . . ."

The Creation account makes mention of God resting. In Genesis 2:2 this rest is *sabbath*, a cessation; in Exodus, the resting which God did is *nuach*, the same word used elsewhere in the Bible to describe an active state of rest, "to come to rest or to be at rest."

---

[11] Associated Press interview, Jan. 16, 1959.

[12] "Why Sunday?" excerpts from the Report of the Commission on the Lord's Day, 1948, issued by the Board of Evangelism and Social Service, United Church of Canada, 1957, p. 32.

For example: in 2 Kings 2:15, "the spirit of Elijah doth rest on Elisha"; in Isaiah 11:2, "the spirit of the Lord shall rest upon him." God's "resting is not the same as 'not working,' " says Oscar Cullmann. ". . . It is more a continuation of God's revelation work that also goes on after the six active days of creation and reaches its highest peak during the earthly life of Christ." [13]

Rest in the Old Testament as a place is metamorphic, for the Hebrews did not conceive of their religion as spatial (although those in the Exodus heading for the Promised Land certainly must have thought of their refuge as being in space). After the captivities and dispersions of later years it became clear that Judaism was becoming a religion in time, with no central rallying point in space. The places of rest in the Old Testament are not literal. When the Psalmist says, "This is my rest [manoach—place or state of rest] for ever: here will I dwell," [14] he is not speaking of a corner of the earth or a far hill or a far heaven; the place is qualitative, with a sense of finality.

The rest which Jesus talks about and promises is much the idea of the rest about which the Psalmist talked. Rest is a spiritual quality, a state of existence, and not merely a fixation in time or space. The various spiritual ideas of rest can combine with the physical concepts, as we shall see. But there are basically two ideas of rest in the New Testament that sum up Jesus' ideas of qualitative or spiritual rest.

They are seen in two words: anapauo and katapauo. The first is found in a verbal and a substantive form in Matthew 11:28, 29, where Jesus said: "Come unto me, all ye that labour and are heavy laden, and I will give you rest. Take my yoke upon you, and learn of me; for I am meek and lowly in heart: and ye shall find rest unto your souls." Jesus promises a rest in the midst of labor, a rest for one's soul, though one is engaged under a yoke in activity. Anapauo means to stop or rest backward—it means to soothe, refresh, retreat or experience an intermission. This rest which Jesus talks about comes from him in the way of strength; he is the source of it and it is sufficient for the hour; it is a peace of mind, we might say in

[13] From the German. Oscar Cullmann, "Sabbat und Sonntag Nach dem Johannesevangelicum," In Memoriam Ernst Lohmeyer, herausgegeben von Werner Schmauch (Stuttgart: Evangelischen Verlagswerk, 1951), p. 128.

[14] Psalm 132:14.

popular terms, or merely new joy, new confidence in the midst of trial, as Jesus also said: "In the world ye shall have tribulation: but be of good cheer; I have overcome the world." [15]

The fact that spiritual rest for the Christian comes from Jesus introduces another facet of it. In the third and fourth chapters of Hebrews *kata* is prefixed to the word, *pauo*, "stop." *"Kata"* gives a certain sense of completeness or inclusiveness to a word; as a preposition, for instance, with *hemera*, "day," *kath' hemeran* becomes "daily." [16] *Katapauo* means to rest permanently, forever. *Katapausis* is a state of final or permanent rest. This is the rest into which the active, faithful Christian enters according to the writer of Hebrews.[17] It is the state of rest that God did enter after the creation.[18] There is a rest prepared for the Christian at the end of his days. Yet there is a rest for him, a refreshment, an *anapausis*, for him, even as he labors. Says a British pastor, the Reverend A. Gilmore, of Northampton, England:

The majority of us today are comparatively well-blessed with holidays, but in addition to the physical renewal which comes from one, two or three weeks away from our work, there is surely another kind of rest that comes to us every day within our work; it comes with the sense of accomplishment and satisfaction. As God looked on the world, saw that it was good, and could then continue working at it, so many a man is able to gaze at his work, know that he has done it well, and find within himself old forces, refreshed and strengthened, that make it possible for him to continue. He has found a rest that is deeper than cessation from labor. It is the rest that God himself knew, and it is God's will that we should know it too.[19]

Rest, then, in the New Testament is not a separation per se, but a permeation, a rest within labor, a peace amid trial, satisfaction in the midst of doing, and this rest in the moment has also eternal significance, for the rest of the Christian is undying; he continues in it beyond death. There is a strong eschatological note in the rest that Jesus gives.

When we consider rest from two standpoints, noticing that there

[15] John 16:33.
[16] Matthew 26:55; Mark 14:49; Luke 9:23; 19:47; 22:53.
[17] Hebrews 3:11, 18; 4:1, 3, 5, 10, 11.
[18] Hebrews 4:4.
[19] A. Gilmore, "The Christian and His Rest," *Sunday Digest*, May 3, 1959, p. 10.

are really two types of rest, one for the body and one for the soul, we find that neither approach takes us to a Sunday one-day observance. Rest in the Space Age is relative directly to the individual, his changing needs, his predicament in a mechanized society; rest for the Christian is strength and assurance amidst the tension of his times.

Now a Christian, being human, must rest physically, too. How do we couple his physical needs with his spiritual needs? Where does recognizing his physical and his spiritual needs, and the type of rest needed to supply both, take us?

Rest in a physical and a spiritual sense might unite in these two ways:

1. *Retreats.* Jesus, although he attended faithfully the religious worship of his time, when he wanted to rest and refresh himself, both physically and spiritually, went off by himself. "And when it was day, he departed and went into a desert place. . . ." [20] "And he withdrew himself into the wilderness, and prayed." [21]

Spiritual retreats have become popular in recent years, in Europe and the United States, ranging from children and family camps to the strongly concentrated spiritual-life weekend conferences of the Episcopalians, the Disciples, Methodists, and others. Both physical rest, getting away from it all, and spiritual rest, being refreshed by the power and spirit of God, are products of these periods of retreat. Without taking offense against the usual church worship, we should note that often the regular service cannot achieve both types of renewal—at best it renews the spirit, but then it often becomes so routine that sometimes the spirit is not renewed either. A pastor calling on one of his parish members asked why he was not at church that morning. The parish member replied: "I'd rather be in bed thinking about church, than in church thinking about bed. At least my mind will be in the right place!"

The retreat idea can occasionally be combined with the regular time of worship and achieve both worship and resting values. The Evangelical Covenant Church in a Midwest community recently announced the next week's service in a Sunday-morning church

---

[20] Luke 4:42.
[21] Luke 5:16.

bulletin: It said: "Next Sunday: SUNDAY SCHOOL PICNIC—10:45.
The picnic will be held at Fabians Park. We will leave the church
at 10:45 promptly. Each family is to bring a covered dish to pass,
a pie, sandwiches and table service for their own family. MORNING
WORSHIP—11:00. There will be special music and congregational
singing led by Bill Martin. Hope to see you there." This is an annual
tradition with this church—the church building is completely shut
down on Sunday morning as all go to the park. Another church in
the same city, the big St. Paul's Evangelical and Reformed Church,
a few weeks later announced that the Sunday-morning service would
not be held. Instead, there would be a 4:00 P.M. vesper service at
the picnic grove. Note the time and place. How shocking, yet is it
not wonderful? I cannot imagine many of our Baptist churches, or
Lutheran or Presbyterian or Methodist, packing up and going to the
park for church. Recently the pastor of the Lutheran church in
Michigan took the men of his church ice fishing on Sunday morning.
His explanation: "I can find nothing wrong with a church or its
appointed ministers unbending to make religion a living, personal
experience." The group, however, did return for the regular worship
in the sanctuary. Also in Michigan, a Lutheran congregation, five
hundred strong, improvised an altar and combined a picnic and the
regular worship service on Bob-Lo Island, near Detroit. It has done
this nine years in a row. Perhaps we ought to see more "unbending" in
the Space Age—at least it is one way of relating the physical and spiritual, of getting the most renewal out of our worship. And there is one
other value in successfully combining rest, spiritually speaking, with
the more mundane things of life, including those that fall into the
area of recreation. The church becomes able to compete with the
other things around it. Whether churches want to go so far as to
put on a "jazz mass," as several Episcopalian churches have done
lately, or experiment with a syncopated beat as a Buffalo Methodist
church did successfully, depends on their tastes, whom they want
to reach, and so on. But a novel combination in our services of religious themes basic to spiritual peace with the various media that
communicate to the audience we are trying to reach might be worth
considering.

The church has gone a long way with camping programs. This
might be a good point to think about more specifically as the church

adapts its worship time to the mentality of the Space Age. Chad Walsh, who has gone so far as to suggest that we consider adapting the monastic idea to the Christian situation, says: "Professor Toynbee has shown the importance of the pattern, 'withdrawal-and-return.' The Christians who withdrew from secular society to found a Christian community would create a new life which would in time spill over the boundaries into the outside world. There are also signs that some churches which have been historically hostile to monasticism are rethinking their attitude toward it. A group of French Protestants, to give one instance, has recently established a monastery near Cluny." [22] Gerald Heard in his book on the Beatitudes also speaks of small Christian retreat fellowships becoming the dynamos to recharge the batteries.[23]

Let us pay great attention to the retreat idea, the one way of realizing the maximum in rest values for our age. And let us not keep the retreat idea entirely for the corporate life of the church, but encourage the idea of retreats within the day's schedule—a walk home from work by a different route, meditating on the relationship of God to the things around us, or a lunch hour alone and in silence, if one is used to the gay group, or if one is withdrawn, reclusive, a lunch hour in fellowship with a group. The idea of retreat works both ways. There is no place that cannot be a retreat, from a home to the noisy subway. I remember in my seminary days, for one Hebrew course I had to learn Hebrew passages by memory. Thus I learned to spend many a moment standing, struggling on the subway train in Chicago, reciting silently the Twenty-third Psalm in Hebrew, a most profitable and satisfying retreat in the daily schedule. Could it be that we in the Space Age should talk more about periods of retreat, a variety of church occasions, a unified, weekly inherent schedule of worship in and out of the church, and less about a single day, a single hour, and a single type of worship?

2. *Activity.* As rest in a physical sense can be achieved amidst activity, so it is in the spiritual sense. Rest in God, peace of mind, hope of salvation come not in inactivity and idleness, but in service.

[22] Chad Walsh, *Early Christians of the Twenty-first Century* (New York: Harper and Brothers, 1949), p. 176.
[23] Gerald Heard, *The Code of Christ: An Interpretation of the Beatitudes* (New York: Harper and Brothers, 1941), p. 147.

Among the Jehovah's Witnesses, each person is a minister. Some are part-time "publishers"; the rest are "pioneers," the full-time workers. The pioneers are expected to work a minimum of one hundred hours a month, ringing doorbells and "placing" items of their fifteen-ton daily output of literature. That is a faith for the Space Age: each person a minister. What is said about a Roman Catholic nun who defected to the Communists should be a challenge to Christians in the Space Age: "Jen Tsong, sister of Han Tai (in Hopeh), works even on Sundays and holy days. In production she is as good as the average male worker. She never loses any time. If she cannot work in the fields, because of rain, she goes out doing propaganda work among Catholics. She was named 'model woman worker' and decorated as such with the 'Flower of Glory.'" [24]

The Christian faith is not a tranquilizer for the busy, hustling American. In fact, it should make him hustle a little bit more, especially in his growing leisure time, for the sake of Christ, and in the midst of his regular hustling it can bring a sense of destiny into his activity. Christ does not bring inactivity to the busy person, or a stalemate of mind; he brings opportunities, challenges.

Billy Graham's tirelessness and eagerness to preach in spite of a nagging physical handicap demanded admiration. Peter Marshall died reasonably young, possibly with overwork contributing to his death. A recent visitor to Albert Schweitzer at Lambaréné, French Equatorial Africa, said: "Here there is no Wednesday afternoon off for golf, no automobile ride into the country Saturday or Sunday." [25] Schweitzer is eighty-four at the time of this writing. These men and others, including the countless army of missionaries and martyrs, know what it is to burn out for Christ; they know how to conserve; yet more important than their conservation and physical renewal is keeping at the job Christ has for them full time. They can say with Paul, "Neither count I my life dear unto myself." [26] They have responded to Paul's plea to the Romans: "I beseech you therefore, brethren, by the mercies of God, that ye present your bodies a living

[24] Sister Superior Suen Tsong-yi of Sienhsien writing in the "Patriotic" Catholic *Review*, published in Tientsin. From a copy received by official Catholic sources in Hong Kong.

[25] E. C. Eastvold (president, Pacific Lutheran College), "Is Albert Schweitzer a Christian?" *Christian Herald*, August, 1959, p. 40.

[26] Acts 20:24.

sacrifice, holy, acceptable unto God, which is your reasonable service." [27] The servants of God ask nothing in return except opportunities to win more to Christ. A tireless vocation.

While the secular man sees only what he needs physically and counts on Sunday to help him accomplish it, the religious man sees that there is a far greater rest. When he considers rest, whether it be a part of or separate from his religious vocation, he does not permit it to become a stop sign or a detour as an end in itself.

As new ideas of rest emerge in the Space Age, it is seen that rest is a part of a total picture, that it is never boredom or inactivity except, perhaps, in the case of sleep. But rest on a conscious level must include an engagement of forces. Sunday cannot really be separated from the balance of life, and the layman who really depends on Sunday for either spiritual or physical rest has no long-range satisfaction. This is where a relevant Christian view of rest merges or at least concurs with the idea of physical rest. Christ brings commitment, enthusiasm, opportunities, satisfaction which a mere preoccupation, such as a hobby or pursuit as an end in itself, does not bring. Christ puts meaning into life, and though a person may wear himself out, and even die younger than if he lived a sub-human, vegetable existence, he achieves a degree of rest and satisfaction for his own body and for his spirit which looks forward to and rejoices in the anticipation of a fulfillment of joy beyond this world.

[27] Romans 12:1.

III WHERE DOES SUNDAY COME FROM?

In the Bible there is no reference to "Sunday," or "day of the Sun." But the other names for this day which appear in our state laws, "the first day of the week," "Sabbath," "The Lord's Day" can be found in the Bible. Whether any of these mean the same as our idea of Sunday, of course, is a question never wholly settled. It is not our purpose to enter into the Seventh-day Adventist and Lord's Day Alliance exchange, where one extreme faces the other. But it does enlighten us, without special interest except that of relevance, to look briefly into the origin of Sunday. By looking at the beginnings of Sunday, one can find help in determining the role of Sunday in the Space Age.

The one-day-out-of-seven idea—Sunday, Sabbath, first day of the week, Lord's day—has roots in pre-Biblical times. The Babylonians, who were moon worshipers, rested on the fifteenth day of the month, the time of the full moon. They called this *shabattu*, meaning "cease," or "rest." Actually the Babylonians are believed to have observed four chief moon days, probably the first, eighth, fifteenth, and twenty-second of each month. Each was called a sabbath because there was a cessation of work to permit the people to celebrate and worship on these days. "Among the Babylonians these seventh days through astrological conceptions became ill-omened, while the sabbath in the middle of the month was made a day of propitiation, and its name was construed as meaning 'the day for ending the wrath of the gods.' The Israelites, on the other hand, made the sabbaths the feast of a living and holy God." [1] The sabbath for the Babylonians was for penance; while to the early Hebrews it was a day of gladness and rest.

The day of the full moon, the fifteenth of the month, continued to be observed by the Jews as a feast day, at least in the seventh month.[2] Both the Sabbath and the day of the new moon were favorite days for consulting the prophets. The husband of the Shunammite woman, when their son was stricken and she proposed to go to Elisha, said: "Why will you go to him today? It is neither new moon, nor sabbath?" [3] And in Amos: "When will the new moon be over, that we may sell grain? and the sabbath, that we may offer wheat for sale?" [4] So the Hebrews kept special biweekly festivals, in addition to breaking the days into seven-day weeks and observing the last day as a day of rest and rejoicing. Jews today still observe a Shabuoth celebration, a Feast of Weeks (*shabuoth* means "weeks") which follows Passover by seven weeks. Originally a day of presenting the first fruits of the harvest as a thank offering in the Temple in Jerusalem, it is now the time of confirmation.

In other parts of the world there were rest days connected with the religious life. Rest days in the animistic religions were linked with festivals and were not on a periodic calendar basis. "These sabbaths were observed at critical times in the lives of the people or of the community, because of such events as an earthquake, a conflagration, an epidemic of sickness, after a death, at the change of the moon, at the end of the old and beginning of the new year, and in connection with such important events as seedtime and harvest and the celebration of solemn ceremony." [5] For example, the Hawaiians simply would leave their tasks and attend the religious session. On special occasions, fires were not lighted, people had to stay in their homes, unless attending religious services; they

[1] Wilhelm P. F. F. Lotz, "Sabbath" in *The New Schaff-Herzog Encyclopedia of Religious Knowledge*, Samuel Macauley Jackson, Editor, Vol. 10 (New York: Funk and Wagnalls Company, 1911), pp. 135, 136.

[2] Leviticus 23:39; Numbers 28:17; 29:12.

[3] 2 Kings 4:23.

[4] Amos 8:5 (RSV). See also Isaiah 1:13; 66:23; Hosea 2:11.

[5] Charles Herbert Huestis, *Sunday in the Making* (New York: Abingdon Press, 1929), p. 26.

were not permitted to bathe or launch a canoe, and the whole community was enjoined to be silent.

Special holy days were evident in later, organized religion. Buddhists observe a sabbath, or Upsosatha. This occurs four times a month—on the day of the full moon, on the day of no moon, and on the two days which are the eighth from the full moon. A number of activities are restricted on these days. Buying and selling are prohibited. Schools and law courts are closed. Even hunting and fishing are forbidden. Muslims place extra emphasis on Friday, as we have seen, the crowning day of creation. They have a sermon on that day and in many areas it is regarded as a sabbath, although the Qur'an prescribes parts of every day as a sabbath, or rather, as worship periods, and encourages buying and selling even on Friday.[6]

As far back as we can go, one fact cannot be ignored: whether the Sabbath is the rest-penance days of the Babylonians or the expression of the superstition and tabu of the most primitive people, or whether we stay with more modern religion, particularly with the Biblical Judaeo-Christian tradition, the sabbath idea is a religious idea.

It has been questioned whether the earliest Hebrews, who were nomads, ever observed a sabbath, for their sheep and cattle would demand care on the seventh as on any other day. But undoubtedly the seventh day was observed before the giving of the Commandments, because the fourth commandment calls upon the people to remember the day and keep it holy. Elsewhere the Mosaic regulations specified what might be done on the Sabbath and what might not be done.

In the creation passages, God rests on the seventh day. But nothing is said about ordering man to keep the day. The first allusion to keeping the Sabbath is in Exodus 16:22: "And it came to pass, that on the sixth day they gathered twice as much bread, two omers for one man . . ." In the Decalogue of Exodus 20, keeping the Sabbath is enjoined as a memorial of creation where God rested

[6] Chapter 62, Al-Jumu'ah, Part 28, Section R.2, verses 10–12. *The Holy Qur'an* (Rabwah, Pakistan: The Oriental and Religious Publishing Corporation, Ltd., 1954), p. 563.

on the seventh day; however, when it is brought into the Deuter-
onomic account,[7] the Sabbath becomes a liberation or independence
day in commemoration of the deliverance of the Jews from Egypt.

Periods of fifty days, or "pentecontads," were originated during
the time of Moses. In each pentecontad were seven weeks of forty-
nine days, including seven sabbaths, with one extra day dedicated
unto the Lord.[8]

It was at a much later date, during the Babylonian captivity, that the
pentecontad plan with its special 50th day was abandoned and a regular
invariable seventh-day Sabbath was introduced, with the Babylonian luni-
solar calendar as its background and framework. At this time the Jewish
religious leaders formulated their theory of the "unbroken continuity of
the seven-day week," maintaining that their new system had started with
the Creation and emphasizing the divine origin of the Sabbath. The Sabbath for the first time became identified with the idea of the unbroken
continuity of the weeks. The simple, divinely inspired seventh day for
worship was now confused with the new idea of the unbroken sequence of
weeks.[9]

For the Jew the weekly Sabbath became one of the pillars of his
religion—the Sabbath plus the rite of circumcision. These two observances were what separated Jews from the Gentile world. The
matter of Sabbath violation was so serious that the penalty was
death.[10]

It is hard to know what Jesus thought of the Sabbath; yet what
he thought is probably clearer on this subject than on others, such
as baptism, holy communion, church unity. His actions showed a
lack of appreciation for the popular uniqueness of the day; eight
times [11] he broke the Jewish regulations by some type of work,

[7] Deuteronomy 5:15.
[8] Leviticus 23:15, 16.
[9] Elizabeth Achelis, *Of Time and the Calendar* (New York: Thomas Nelson
and Sons taking over the title originally published by Hermitage House, 1955),
pp. 87, 88.
[10] Numbers 15:35.
[11] (1) Healing of the man with the unclean spirit at Capernaum—Mark
1:21–27; Luke 4:33–37; (2) Healing of Peter's mother-in-law on the same day
—Mark 1:29–32; Matt. 8:14, 15; Luke 4:35–40; (3) Healing of the infirm man
at the pool of Bethesada—John 5:5–18; (4) Plucking the ears of corn—Mark
2:23–28; Matt. 12:1–8; Luke 6:1–5; (5) Healing of the man with the withered
hand—Mark 3:1–5; Matt. 12:9–14; Luke 6:6–11; (6) Healing the blind man

charitable or otherwise. He was not secretive about it. He healed
the infirm man at the Pool of Bethesda in the shadow of the Temple;
he permitted his disciples to pluck corn under the very noses of the
Pharisees; in Galilee he deliberately healed the man with the withered hand in the synagogue as "they [the Pharisees] watched him."
Jesus openly defied the Sabbath customs. Yet in his early ministry
it was his custom to go up to the synagogue on the Sabbath.[12] But
even this custom had some very unorthodox overtones. In the
synagogue on a Sabbath he declared himself the deliverer of his
people, and before he had finished his utterances the worshipers
were intent upon heaving him over a cliff. Whether his custom remained the same after that is not known, but he did not return
to his home synagogue again. The fact that Jesus attended the
synagogue on a definite day does not commit him to that day or
a substitute for that day. If he did not attend on the Sabbath, when
would he attend? It is quite possible he had his own preference, not
necessarily precluded by his action.

Jesus' chief interest was the inner life of man—he was not concerned with the outside of the cup if the inner man was cleansed
and made new. He healed where there was faith [13] or he healed
with the view of increasing the faith of those about him.[14] Except
as they touched the spirit of man He was not concerned with dogma,
the accepted customs, the current rituals, and the great intricacies
of the commentaries on the law. He had come not to destroy the
law, but to fulfill it; not to alter one dot or one little stroke in the
letters of the law. This was really outside his vocation. He was
God's son—a teacher from God, not a Temple rabbi bent on inter-
preting the interpretations of the law. Being from God, Jesus' concern was the spiritual welfare of man, "The sabbath was made for
man, and not man for the sabbath." [15] He did not deny the Sabbath's significance in the Hebrew religion, nor did he encourage it,
although some might draw the inference that because the disciples

---

at the Pool of Siloam—John 9:11–38; (7) Healing of the woman with a spirit
of infirmity—Luke 13:11–17; (8) Healing the man with dropsy—Luke 14:1–6.
  [12] Luke 4:16–30; Mark 6:1–6.
  [13] Matthew 8:10; Mark 9:24.
  [14] John 6:14; 9:1–38; 11:26, 27, 45; 12:37.
  [15] Mark 2:27.

continued observing the Sabbath their Jewish Master must have,
too. We can say by an ingenious compilation of prooftexts that he
reaffirmed that day of creation, or on the other hand that he trans-
posed that day to the first day of the week. But the truth of the matter is that Jesus was not concerned with that day per se. His religion
is a far deeper thing than the endorsement or the interruption of a
calendar. "For I say unto you," said Jesus, "That except your
righteousness shall exceed the righteousness of the scribes and
Pharisees, ye shall in no case enter into the kingdom of heaven." [16]
Jesus told the Pharisees: "Ye . . . have omitted the weightier matters of the law, judgment, mercy, and faith." [17]

In the Sermon on the Mount, Jesus comments on many of the
Hebrew laws, both covenant and ceremonial. Each time he moves
on to another law, he states authoritatively, "Ye have heard that it
has been said." Then, "but I say unto you." The Jews in the old
times were taught a law of retaliation, an eye for an eye and a tooth
for a tooth—Jesus reverses this. He says, "Love your enemies"—
even "bless them that curse you," even "pray for them which de-
spitefully use you, and persecute you." [18] Jesus' religion was beyond
the law, deeper than it, more inclusive, beyond contradiction. What
would he say about the Sabbath? What did he say about the other
laws? Concerning the Ten Commandments, he had two suggestions:
(1) Go beyond them; for instance, in reference to adultery, he said,
do not even harbor illicit thoughts.[19] (2) Generally, concerning the
Commandments, he said "love God" and "love your neighbor"—on
these hang all the laws.[20] Where does the Sabbath fit in? Is it not
tenable to emphasize that Jesus preferred each day as a holy day,
letting Sabbath theology fall where it may?

In one of the oldest New Testament manuscripts, Codex Bezae,
there is inserted after Luke 6:5 this additional quotation attributed
to Jesus, which, because it was not included in other acceptable
texts, is left out of our Bibles: "On the same day, seeing one working on the Sabbath, he said unto him, O man, if indeed thou know-

[16] Matthew 5:20.
[17] Matthew 23:23.
[18] Matthew 5:44.
[19] Matthew 5:28.
[20] Matthew 22:37–40.

est what thou doest, thou art blessed; but if thou knowest not, thou are accursed and a transgressor of the law." These words would have Jesus condoning Sabbath breaking if done under a higher motivation. For those under the law, a willful breaking of the fourth commandment is bad. This seems to be consistent with the accepted Gospel record, that when Jesus or any of his disciples, consciously or unconsciously felt a compulsion to break the Sabbath, as long as they did it in a clear conscience they had the privilege of living above the traditional commandments. This was not antinomianism, for freedom in Christ, a new birth, was not freedom for moral disintegration but rather a freedom in terms of responsibility.

The Sabbath was not strictly a rest day for Jesus. He taught in the synagogues, on the hills, on the sea.[21] He continued his work of healing and preaching.[22] Jesus did not depend on his Sabbath for his rest, any more than a minister of the Gospel or a Sunday-school teacher or any church worker does today. Jesus had his own concept of rest. "And he said unto them, Come ye yourselves apart into a desert place, and rest a while: for there were many coming and going, and they had no leisure so much as to eat. And they departed into a desert place by ship privately." [23] If this was a part of a schedule, measured by a solar or lunar or Hebrew calendar, we do not know it. Jesus, being physical, sought his rest. He needed it, and received it—physically in retirement and spiritually in communion with his Father.

All four Gospels, as they draw to a close, introduce another day of the week. They speak of "the first day of the week" as the time the women came to the tomb. Unable to buy spices on the Sabbath, they did so immediately upon sunset Saturday which ended the Jewish Sabbath.[24] The sun was already up when they gathered at the tomb. For forty days Jesus continues to make appearances to his

[21] Mark 2:1, 2, 7.

[22] His schedule, however, was probably relieved somewhat on this day. In the house of Peter, Jesus healed Peter's mother-in-law on the Sabbath, but it was not until after sunset, the end of the Sabbath, that the crowds came with their sick (Mark 1:32).

[23] Mark 6:31, 32.

[24] Luke 23:56 seems to vary from Mark 16:1 at this point; Mark says that the Sabbath was past when the spices were bought; Luke said they were prepared, and then the women rested on the Sabbath.

followers,[25] but Luke prefers to mention in detail only the events that happen on the first day of the week. For example, in starting the account of the Emmaus road incident, he says, "two of them were going that very day to a village named Emmaus," [26] and the transition to the upper room occurs immediately on the heels of this incident—"And they rose up the same hour, and returned to Jerusalem, and found the eleven gathered together." [27] John further emphasizes the first day of the week by not only indicating that the tomb was found empty on that day but also by reporting the appearances of Jesus to his disciples on two Sundays in a row.[28] This second appearance to the disciples in the upper room was "after eight days." Thus presuming that both Sundays were counted, this meant that Jesus appeared on two successive Sundays. The next appearance recorded by John probably occurred during the week. The disciples had gone fishing, "and that night they took nothing." [29] The day is not mentioned. If they had begun fishing before dark, and this appearance at daybreak was on the first day of the week, then the disciples would have had to start their fishing on the Sabbath. Possibly if it had been on the first day or some other day in relationship to the Sabbath, the day before, for instance, or on some holy day, John would have mentioned it.

What then is the reason for the emphasis on the first day of the week? Why do Luke and John, when they date Christ's appearances, date only those that occur on the first day? Perhaps these are literal dates, and the writers are merely reporting the exact times when the events happened. This is what the author prefers to think, without making a case for one day or another out of it. Possibly the writers are attempting to pinpoint the activity which followed the holy, important day of rest with the effect "immediately after the Sabbath." Again, perhaps Luke and John by their selective chronology were trying to say that the early church had come to a particular distinctiveness in regard to this day. But as far as the Gospels are concerned there is nothing directly in the words of Jesus or in

[25] Acts 1:3.
[26] Luke 24:13.
[27] Luke 24:33.
[28] John 21:26.
[29] John 21:4.

the words of the Gospel writers which engenders reverence for the first day of the week. There is simply a reporting of the things that happened.

John, in his Apocalypse, introduces the term (*kyriake hemera*) "the Lord's day," or literally in the Greek, "the day pertaining to the Lord." This is an unusual usage in the light of both the Septuagint (Greek Old Testament) and the Greek New Testament. Throughout the Septuagint and the New Testament, a possessive (or genitive) is used—*hemera kyriou*, literally "Lord's day" and with definite articles, *te hemera tou kyriou*, literally "the day of the Lord." Actually both are used for the coming Day of the Lord.[30]

The word *kyriake* appears once earlier in the New Testament in 1 Corinthians 11:20 in reference to the "Lord's Supper," but never is it used in reference to the Lord's Day except by John. What does it mean in the Book of Revelation? John uses very strange grammatical constructions throughout his Apocalypse (due possibly to the apocalyptic subject, his own old age, the lack of copy editors on the isle of Patmos for this language which is not his native tongue, and so on) John felt that the day was peculiar to the Lord. But he does not say which day it was, and even if it could be decided that he meant a Sabbath or a first day, whether he considered the day unique is not indicated. Emil G. Hirsch, in *The Jewish Encyclopedia*, suggests that it may be translated "the Day of the Lord," just as the other forms of "Lord's Day" mentioned above may be.[31]

Possibly the term *he kyriake hemera* was beginning to come into vogue at the time John wrote at the close of the first century. Later writers used a shortened term, *he kyriake*. This Ignatius did in his letter to the Magnesians, around A.D. 110. He spoke of Jewish Christians as "no longer observing the Sabbath but living after [or in or during] the Lord's Day [*kyriake* only—the word for day is missing] in which our life also rose through him and through his death." [32]

---

[30] Lord's Day (*hemera kyriou*) in 1 Thess. 5:2 and 2 Peter 3:10; The Day of the Lord (*te hemera tou kyriou*) in 1 Cor. 5:5 and 2 Cor. 1:14. All of these are translated the same in both the King James and the Revised Standard Version—"The Day of the Lord." Thus the day which the Lord actually possesses, in the Greek, is the eschatological or final Day of the Lord.

[31] Emil G. Hirsch, "Sabbath and Sunday" in *The Jewish Encyclopedia*, Isidore Singer, editor, Vol. 10 (New York: Funk and Wagnalls Company, 1905), p. 604.

[32] From the Greek text in P. T. Camelot's *Ignace D'Antioche, Lettres,* "Aux Magnesiens," Chap. 9, Verse 1 (Paris: Editions du Cerf, 1944), p. 6.

Similarly the *Didache,* or "Teaching," of the twelve apostles, composed early in the second century, employs the shorter form: "On the Lord's own day, having assembled together, break bread and offer thanks, first confessing your sins, so that your sacrifice might be clean." [33]

Thus the Lord's Day idea was becoming familiar in the second century, to the extent that a shortened form was used. Language can be a clue to the origin and acceptability of a term. Titles and official designations shorten with familiarity. Consider our abbreviations and our slang. Possibly the term *kyriake hemera* was not only new and unique in the Bible, appearing only in the final Apocalypse written at the close of the first century, but also new in the life of the church, with familiarity growing in the subsequent years and centuries, as *kyriake* becomes a popular idiom without the word "day" (*hemera*).

When John speaks of the Lord's Day in his Apocalypse he shows a reaction to the familiar custom of celebrating the Emperor's Day, or the first day of every month in honor of the emperor. The word *kyriake* properly referred to the emperor, meaning "imperial." Would it be that John wanted to emphasize his allegiance to the Lord by declaring that this certain time was the Lord's day, not the emperor's day?

Then again, it is possible that he wanted to get some other meaning across, as his whole statement is imbedded in imagery. He says: "I was in the Spirit on the Lord's day, and heard behind me a great voice, as of a trumpet . . ." It is within reason that the Lord's day is symbolic, just as the "voice" or "trumpet." He is using the emperor's terminology, possibly cryptically to pass the censors, and/or symbolically to contrast the day with the emperor's day. But if so, what day did he originally mean—an eschatological, a here-and-now, or a futuristic day of the Lord, or the first day of the month or week?

What Paul says about the Sabbath or a Lord's day, like the teachings of Jesus, is indirect. The Adventists like the fact that Paul was

---

[33] From the Greek text, Chap. 14, Verse 1, in T. W. Crafer's *The Teaching of the Twelve Apostles* (New York: The Macmillan Company, 1920), p. 14.

"The Lord's own day" is a pleonastic arrangement, literally "the Lord's Lord's (day)" (*kata kyriaken kyriou*), perhaps for emphasis.

faithful in his Sabbath worship. On the other hand, the Lord's Day people like the fact that he bubbled over in a new spirit and new life in Christ, with great sermons at Athens and in his Epistles on the resurrection, such as 1 Corinthians 15. Thus for them, Paul, because he emphasized the resurrection, would be in favor of a Lord's day or Sunday observance. But this is special pleading. Paul never gave the slightest indication of linking the resurrection to a special resurrection-day observance, any more than he did with the cross, concerning which he also had much to say.

Building arguments as to which day is the Lord's stands in opposition to what Paul is trying to say. Verbal contentions are contrary to the Gospel. Jesus came, not to bring the birth of new dogmas, but to bring about the birth of new persons in the Spirit. Thus Paul warns: "Avoid foolish questions, and genealogies, and contentions, and strivings about the law; for they are unprofitable and vain." [34]

Paul's ministry is the story of a fugitive, courageously challenging and evading the representatives of the Jewish law. After his conversion, to escape the Jewish authorities, Paul had to be let down from the wall of Damascus in a basket under the cover of night. From town to town across Asia Minor, Macedonia, Achaia, Paul is hounded by Jews, some of them authorities, some of them "vagabonds," as in Ephesus and, earlier, at Lystra, where itinerant Jews who had come from Antioch and Iconium incited the people to pelt him with stones.

Nevertheless, Paul continually seeks out Jewish groups on the Sabbath, reasons with them as in Corinth, worships with them as with Lydia and her friends in or near Philippi. There no synagogue existed. The devout Jews sought specific places for meeting and worship. The place at Philippi was by a river. Paul's desire, however, was not to reengage their enthusiasm for the law, but to bring them the good news of the Savior, the Messiah.

To the new Christians at Colosse he wrote that the ordinances were blotted out, as though nailed to the cross. He continued: "Let no man therefore judge you in meat, or in drink, or in respect of an holyday, or of the new moon, or of the sabbath days: Which are

[34] Titus 3:9.

a shadow of things to come; but the body is of Christ." [35] Paul's attitude toward the Sabbath resembles his attitude toward the whole law. "Paul apparently did not consider it [the Sabbath] a Christian institution, but part of the Mosaic law abolished in Christ (Romans 14:5, Col. 2:16). His view was recovered at the Reformation. William Tyndale wrote: 'We be lords over the sabbath and may yet change it into the Monday, or any other day, as we see need; or may make every tenth day holy day only, if we see a cause why. We may make two every week, if it were expedient, and one not enough to teach the people.'" [36] Paul's view, after it was regained, was obscured in the seventeenth century by the Puritans, never to be fully recovered by the church, although approximated by the spiritual descendants of Luther in his emphasis on Christian liberty.

The meeting time of the early church, as recorded in Acts, is difficult to pinpoint. Those who are familiar with A. T. Robertson's popular *A Harmony of the Gospels* know that he gives two possible days for many of the activities in the last week of the life of Christ. The anointing of Jesus' feet by Mary of Bethany, Robertson places on Tuesday evening, or Jewish Wednesday; the paschal meal, on Thursday evening after sunset or beginning of Jewish Friday, and so on for each of the evening occasions. The reason for this is the fact that the Jews reckoned their day beginning at sunset and ending at sunset of the next day. A day could begin hours earlier in a valley than on a mountaintop. This peculiar relativity of time and reckoning of the day by the setting of the sun is strange to our minds. For example, who would think that a snack at four-thirty in the afternoon, or even a coffee break in the middle of an afternoon in Alaska, is really breakfast of the next day? But this arrangement of days is a factor to be considered in understanding the Jewish reckoning of time as used in the Book of Acts. In Acts 20:7 Paul is in Troas. "And upon the first day of the week, when the disciples came together to break bread, Paul preached unto them, ready to depart on the morrow; and continued his speech until midnight." The word "day" does not appear in the Greek text; the word for "week" here is the same as "Sabbath" and the whole

[35] Colossians 2:16, 17.
[36] Henry Sloane Coffin, Exposition of Isaiah 40—66 in *The Interpreter's Bible*, Vol. V (New York: Abingdon Press, 1956), p. 655.

phrase could very well be translated literally as "upon the first of the Sabbaths." But we shall assume, with most translators past and present (Calvin is an exception), that "day" should be inserted and "Sabbaths" translated "week" on the basis that this comes from a Hebrew and Aramaic idiom of time. But when did this first day begin? "Was the time Saturday evening—the 'first day' on Jewish methods of calculation beginning at what we would call 6 P.M. on Saturday—or Sunday evening?" asks Theodore P. Ferris, rector of Trinity Church, Boston, in *The Interpreter's Bible*. "Almost certainly the latter, as the morrow, when Paul intended to depart, most naturally means the day after that first mentioned, and therefore is presumably Monday." [37] But even then, the verse is not without problems. For if Paul preached (Greek—"conversed," or "carried on a dialogue") until midnight on our Sunday, then at least six hours of this "first day" meeting was on Monday. If he began his preaching sometime on the first day (before 6:00 P.M. Sunday), then Paul must have had a lot to say, a prolific conversation that could not have been less than six hours or so in length if he continued to midnight. Even after midnight he talked a long time, with an interruption to pick up Eutychus who had fallen from a window. "When he therefore was come up again, and had broken bread, and eaten, and talked a long while, even till break of day, so he departed." [38]

What is the significance of this first day in Acts 20:7? Paul gives his last speech—surely it is not his only speech or sermon to the church in his stay of seven days there.[39] No doubt the days were packed with speeches, formal and conversational. Along with the early routine of daily breaking bread we read also that those that were being saved were added to the church daily.[40] And if the proclamation of the *kerygma* or message of the Gospel is as necessary to the faith as most modern theologians from Lutheran Rudolf Bultmann, with his exaggerated existentialism, to Reformed thinker Karl Barth, with his neo-Calvinism, think it is, no doubt the daily

[37] Theodore P. Ferris, Exposition of Acts, in *The Interpreter's Bible*, Vol. 9 (New York: Abingdon-Cokesbury Press, 1954), p. 267.
[38] Acts 20:11.
[39] Acts 20:6.
[40] Acts 2:47.

breaking of bread included proclamations of the faith. So what was really unique about this meeting? Nothing, really, except that Paul was leaving on the morrow, and his speaking, or at least the service in its entirety, lasted into two days, either Saturday and Sunday, or Sunday and Monday.

On one occasion, Paul makes reference to the first day of the week. In his second epistle to the Corinthians, Paul recommends a pattern of receiving money as used by the churches in Galatia. "Upon the first day of the week let every one of you lay by him in store, as God hath prospered him, that there be no gatherings when I come." [41] Most scholars accept the translation, "the first day of the week," but, as in the other "first day" references, the Greek does not contain the word "day," and there are some alternative translations, such as "upon the first of the week" or "upon or during Sabbath's one or first hour, day, and so on," or as Calvin preferred: "On one of the Sabbaths." [42] It is not clear what Paul had in mind. Was he thinking of only one collection to be taken in the course of a meeting or a Sabbath day, or was it generally at the first of one week in particular and each week which followed? Or if the phrase is taken as it is traditionally supposed: "on the first day of the week," what sanction does this special first-day offering give in setting aside the first day as a special holy day on a par with or as a replacement for the Jewish Sabbath?

Over against the seven mentions of the first day of the week in the New Testament (five in connection with the resurrection account in the Gospels, one in Acts 20:7 and another in 1 Corinthians 16:2) and one reference to a Lord's Day in Revelation—all raising questions in context and translations—there are 84 references to the Sabbath in Acts alone. The Adventists like this. Sheer weight of numbers is on their side. But that is no way to read the Bible, as Herbert S. Bird in *Christianity Today* points out:

The Adventists handle the evidence in such cavalier fashion that it becomes difficult to credit them with holding such views in all seriousness. Consider, for example, their frequently made assertion that the Book of

[41] 1 Corinthians 16:2.
[42] John Calvin, *Commentary on the Epistles of Paul the Apostle to the Corinthians*, tr. by John Pringle (Grand Rapids, Mich.: William B. Eerdmans, 1948), p. 68.

Acts records 84 Sabbath services and only one first-day service. Certainly their writers cannot be unaware of the fact that all of these 'Sabbath services' were Jewish synagogue meetings at which Christian missionaries appeared in order to preach the Gospel to the Jews, and were not Christian meetings for worship at all. Nor can it have entirely escaped their attention that the New Testament contains no record whatsoever of a Christian Church service that was held on a Saturday. Over against the stress which Adventism places on this point, we have here a silence that is eloquent indeed.[43]

The Scriptures are very disappointing—if we seek to pluck sanctions for Sunday or Saturday from the words and actions of our Savior or from Paul, the Gospels, the Acts of the Apostles, the Epistles, or the Apocalypse. If, on the other hand, our motive is to capture the faith, and its meaning for the times, rather than argue for or against a religious observance, the Scriptures speak with clarity and significance.

We have not answered our question. Just how did we get our Sunday? From the earliest rituals of the Christians to the time of Constantine, there are factors that directly shape the first day of the week as a special Christian day.

Let it be emphasized that the earliest Christians worshiped as Jews. They knew no other way of worship. Jesus himself, brought up in a Jewish home, lived within the framework of the Jewish pattern. The disciples, too, were presumably all Jews. Thus Temple worship,[44] along with the daily customs of breaking bread (and possibly other practices such as preaching, singing, laying on of hands, reading Scripture) comprised the Christian worship pattern. Many of the features of Sunday church are to this day decidedly Jewish—women keeping silence in the Temple, standing at least for part of the service, reading of Scripture, sermons, the offering up of prayers by a minister, the mass with its perpetual administration of the Sacrifice. Characteristics of our Sunday came from Judaism, whether the philosophy of the day did or did not. Sunday began in Judaism.

[43] Herbert S. Bird, "Reply to an Adventist," in *Christianity Today*, Aug. 18, 1958, p. 24.
[44] Acts 3:1.

But Sunday as a new day really emerged because of an attempt not to approximate the Sabbath, but to get away from it. Sunday, or the first day of the week, arose as an antithesis to the Sabbath. After the Council in Jerusalem, it became clear that the official center of Christendom, Jerusalem, would give its sanction to world evangelization of the Gentiles, even as Jesus had commanded.[45] It became inevitable that the leadership of the church would eventually come from outside Jerusalem. Christianity became cosmopolitan, geographically, and in regard to its constituency.

There was a pulling away from the strict orthodoxy. But this was more than a drift away from Judaism. There was a desire to get as far away from Judaism as possible, in spite of the conservative forces that first held the two together. Actually Christians stood at a different pole from the Jews—one tended to be a religion of works, the other of grace. But the parting of the ways did not rise in the differences, for if such were the case Jews and Christians could resolve much of the differences by compromise. The division was heightened by the sameness of their claims. One held that salvation rested within a certain framework for a certain people, the chosen seed of Abraham—the other held that its group represented the chosen children of God in grace. Both claimed to be exclusively the object of God's grace. Like two children with the same possession, such as candy desired by both of them, dissension was bound to develop.

Not helping the situation any was the fact that the Jews persecuted the Christians. The persecution of Paul and his companions by the Jews recorded in the Book of Acts did not end, but continued. Jews assisted in the martyrdom of Polycarp:

The entire crowd of heathen and Jews who lived in Smyrna shouted with uncontrollable anger and a great cry: "This one is the teacher of Asia, the father of Christians, the destroyer of our gods, who teaches many not to sacrifice nor to worship." Such things they shouted and asked the Asiarch Philip that he let loose a lion on Polycarp. . . . Then they decided to shout with one accord that he burn Polycarp alive.[46]

[45] Acts 1:8.
[46] "Martyrdom of Polycarp," from the *Library of Christian Classics*, Vol. I, Cyril C. Richardson, translator and editor (Philadelphia: The Westminster Press, 1953), p. 153.

The Jews then gathered faggots zealously. According to Tertullian, Jewish synagogues were "fountains of persecution." [47]

Practical matters enter the picture more and more to push Christians further away from the Sabbath. The disassociation from Judaism became especially desirable when vicious persecutions developed against the Jews, such as in Caesarea, where all the Jews were killed by the citizenry shortly before the Fall of Jerusalem in A.D. 70 and also during the expulsion of Jews from Rome by Hadrian in A.D. 132. It was dangerous enough to be a Christian, but on certain occasions and in certain localities it was even worse to be a Jew.

The Maccabaean spirit of the Jews in the second century before Christ had carried over into the second century after Christ. The Christians on the other hand were not basically a militant people. When a three-year uprising by the Jews was put down by the Romans in A.D. 135, the Holy City became forbidden to the Jews, but not to the Christians, who had not taken part in the conflict. Certainly the breach with Judaism was desirable, at least on the surface, by this date. There was no need to be Jewish—why should Christians risk their necks as Jews? They were Christians, willing to die as Christians, but not as Jews. Thus a separate day of worship and a growing failure to keep the Jewish Sabbath, as well as the circumcision rites, made it plain that the Christians were not merely Jewish proselytes.

Many of the pagans, who were flocking into church membership from all parts of the world, had come from a sun-worshiping background. Remember, the Jewish religion was as foreign to them as paganism with its idol worship and eating of unclean meats was foreign to Judaism. Sun worship was the chief feature of many pagan cults in the first century, particularly Mithraism. The sun was a common denominator of Middle Eastern religion as well as that of other parts of the world: for example, the battle of Ormazd, the spirit of light and life, with the spirit of darkness, in the Zoroastrian religion, and the yin and yang principles of heaven and earth in the Far Eastern religions. The light of the sun is vivid

---

[47] Tertullian, *Scorpiace,* Chap. 10, in *The Ante-Nicene Fathers,* edited by Alexander Roberts and James Donaldson, Vol. III (New York: Charles Scribner's Sons, 1908), p. 643.

imagery in both the Old and New Testaments, from the creation
account where "the Spirit of God moved upon the face of the waters"
and said, "Let there be light," [48] and when "God planted a garden
eastward in Eden," [49] to the references in prophetic literature, such
as in Malachi ("Unto you that fear my name shall the Sun of righteousness arise with healing in his wings"),[50] to Jesus' reference to
himself as the light of the world [51] to the final verdict that the new
Holy City shall have "no need of the sun." [52] The people of the Dead
Sea Scrolls, the Sabbath-observing Essenes, in their ritual, almost
at the very doorstep of Jerusalem, prayed to the sun at dawn. Sun
worship entered Christianity directly through a number of heretical
sects, and they must have been powerful fads of the time. One of
these was the Manichaean heresy, whose adherents believed that
Jesus was the visible image of the sun. Augustine belonged to this
sect for nine years before he finally renounced it. His continued
debate with them was interesting. He later wrote to one of their
members, Faustus, who had been his tutor: "You are in the habit of
worshiping the sun on what you call Sunday. What you call Sunday
we call the Lord's Day, and on it we do not worship the sun, but
commemorate the Lord's resurrection." [53] This was written at the
beginning of the fifth century, long after Sunday had become official
as a Christian worship day in the Empire. Sun worship was not
without influence.

The "many lights" in the Acts 20 account of the Christian worship at Troas on the first day may have some significance traceable
to the importance of light and the sun in the ancient world, symbolic
perhaps of Jesus' own references to himself and his followers as the
light of the world. The light of the sun was under consideration in
building synagogues and Christian churches. The tabernacle and
the Temple faced east. Jewish synagogues and even many of the

[48] Genesis 1:2, 3.
[49] Genesis 2:8.
[50] Malachi 4:2.
[51] John 8:12.
[52] Revelation 21:23.
[53] Augustine, "Reply to Faustus," Book 18: Chap. 5, quoted in *The Nicene
and Post-Nicene Fathers*, Vol. IV, Philip Schaff, editor (New York: Charles
Scribner's Sons, 1907), p. 238.

early Christian churches were built facing east, not to honor the sun, but, especially in regard to the Jews, to face the Holy Land. The Christian custom of doing this is probably better explained in terms of the many new converts coming from varying backgrounds of sun worship—Roman, Alexandrian, or Near Eastern, or Persian.

When, for example, the basilica was constructed at Rome on the Vatican hill over St. Peter's tomb by the Emperor Constantine I in the fourth century, it had the great doors of the porch facing east, so that the rays of the rising Sun at the equinox passed through the outer and inner doors and the naves until they illuminated the High Altar. The majestic church of St. Peter's completed on the site in the seventeenth century follows the same directional conditions in the design to face the rising Sun at the equinox. This was common in the earliest Christian churches, the priest at the altar facing the worshippers and the Sun while the congregation had their backs to it.[54]

As the Jewish Christians reacted against their legalism and the Jewish Sabbath, moving away from their old day into a new, but nevertheless retaining much of the old worship, so it could have been with the new pagan Christians. They abhorred the things of the past, but it was impossible for them to break away entirely. That which could be assimilated without violation of their new faith, and particularly that which could be recommended as consistent with Jewish-Christian practice, would naturally be well received. Thus the Jewish Christians and Christians from pagan backgrounds both had their practical motives for giving some emphasis to Sunday, or the first day of the week, in their worship calendar.

Convenience was a factor in the rise of the priority of the first day. The earliest Christians were busy with their Jewish duties and requirements on the Sabbath day. But when the day came to a close, they made it a point to come together. That Christians actually did meet on the evenings after the Sabbath (Jewish first day of the week) is shown by Sozomen, who was writing at the end of the

[54] Sir Richard Gregory, *Gods and Men* (London: Stuart and Richards, 1949), p. 85.

fourth century. "The people of Constantinople, and of several other cities, assemble together on the sabbath, as well as on the next day; which custom is never observed at Rome or at Alexandria. There are several cities and villages in Egypt where, contrary to the usages established elsewhere, the people meet together on Sabbath evenings. . . ." [55]

There were, of course, strong theological motives for taking the first day of the week. It was the day of the resurrection, and emphasis on this day could highlight the grace, freedom, and new life in Christ as against the old man, the old way, the old regulations under Moses and the law. To the credit of the first day was not only the fact that the resurrection was unique in the Christian faith, but there was the extra emphasis given to the first day in the reporting of Luke and John. There were reasons for looking toward the first day of the week.

There were reasons for looking toward other days, too. The day of the resurrection was not the only significant day which caught the attention of the early Christians. They could not overlook Christ's sacrifice for them on the cross. This above all things Jesus seemed to want his disciples to remember. When he instituted the Lord's Supper for his followers, he said: "Take, eat: this is my body, which is broken for you: this do in remembrance of me. . . . For as often as ye eat this bread, and drink this cup, ye do shew the Lord's death till he come." [56]

The early Christians made every effort to remember his death, even to the point of breaking bread daily. It is not surprising that certain Jewish elements would also enter into the picture to influence the Christian worship in respect to the death of Christ. The Jews had their fast days on Monday and Thursday, and the first Christians took over these and other observances commemorating calamities in Jewish history. But the Christians had certain calamities of their own that they wanted to commemorate. They chose two special fast days: Wednesday the day Jesus was betrayed, and Friday, the day he was crucified. These two holy days were observed

[55] Edward Welferd, translator, *The Ecclesiastical History of Sozomen* (London: Henry G. Bohn, 1855), Book VII, Chap. 19, p. 344.
[56] 1 Corinthians 11:24, 26.

widely throughout the early church according to Clement of Alexandria,[57] Tertullian,[58] and Augustine.[59]

In the second century, the practice of daily worship and breaking of bread among the early Christians had narrowed to three chief days—Friday, the fast day commemorating the calamity of crucifixion; Saturday, the Jewish Sabbath commemorating the creation and exodus, continued particularly by Jewish Christians in the East; Sunday, the first day of the week, commemorating the resurrection.

It was in the middle of the second century that the first day of the week, which had come to be called the Lord's Day by Ignatius and by the writer of the *Didache*, was first called the day of the Sun, or Sunday by Christians. The first use of this pagan designation in Christian literature is found in Justin Martyr. "We hold this common gathering on Sunday, since it is the first day, on which God transforming darkness and matter made the universe, and Jesus Christ our Savior rose from the dead on the same day. For they crucified him on the day before Saturday, and on the day after Saturday, he appeared to his apostles and disciples and taught them these things which I have passed on to you also for your serious consideration." [60]

Yet this growing emphasis on the Lord's Day, now known as the day of the Sun, by the Christians between the middle of the second and the early part of the fourth century, had not eclipsed the daily worship habits of the Christians. The author of the *Constitutions of the Holy Apostles*, writing in the third century, gives an account of contemporary church life which he claims had been handed down from Apostolic times. He says:

[57] Wilson, William, translator, *The Writings of Clement of Alexandria*, Vol. II, in the *Ante-Nicene Christian Library*, Vol. XII, edited by Alexander Roberts, and James Donaldson (Edinburgh: T. and T. Clark, 1869), The Miscellanies (or Stromata) Book VII, Chap. 12, p. 461.

[58] *The Writings of Tertullian*, Vol. III, *ibid.*, 1870, Vol. XVIII, "On Fasting," Chap. 14, pp. 147–148.

[59] Cunningham, J. G., *The Letters of St. Augustine* in *A Select Library of the Nicene and Post-Nicene Fathers*, Philip Schaff, editor (Buffalo: The Christian Literature Co., 1886), Vol. I, Letter 36, Chap. 13, Number 30, pp. 269–270.

[60] Library of Christian Classics, Justin Martyr, *Apology*, I, 67, *op. cit.*, pp. 287, 288.

. . . assemble yourselves together every day, morning and evening, sing-ing psalms and praying in the Lord's house: in the morning saying the sixty-second Psalm, and in the evening the hundred and fortieth, but principally on the Sabbath-day. And on the day of our Lord's resurrection, which is the Lord's day, meet more diligently, sending praise to God that made the universe by Jesus, and sent Him to us, and condescended to let Him suffer, and raised Him from the dead.[61]

Tertullian, Cyprian and Origen speak of daily times of prayer. Tertullian talks of prayer for the third, sixth, and ninth hours; these he insisted should be definitely apart from the regular prayers, which without specific reminders should come every morning and every evening.

Constantine's own preferences reflect the combination of wor-ship customs that go back to the very beginning of the church. Worship was a daily affair for him. If Eusebius is correct, "The emperor himself, as a sharer in the holy mysteries of our religion, would seclude himself daily at a stated hour in the innermost cham-bers of his place." [62] Constantine also commanded the governors of every province to "respect the days commemorative of martyrs, and duly to honor the festal seasons in the churches; and all these intentions were fulfilled to the emperor's entire satisfaction." [63]

The emperor recognized three special days—Friday, Saturday, and Sunday, with special attention to Friday and Sunday. "Accord-ingly he enjoined on all the subjects of the Roman Empire to observe the Lord's day, as a day of rest, and also to honor the day which precedes the Sabbath (that is, Friday), in memory, I suppose, of what the Saviour of mankind is recorded to have achieved on that day." [64] The Sabbath, nevertheless, was still held in considerable prominence, for also in the fourth century Gregory of Nyssa still spoke of the Sabbath and the Lord's day as sisters. The Council of Laodicea in 363 while condemning a like Jewish observance of

[61] "Constitutions of the Holy Apostles," Book II, Section 7, lix, *The Ante-Nicene Fathers*, Vol. VII, edited by Alexander Roberts and James Donaldson (New York: Charles Scribner's Sons, 1907), p. 423.

[62] Eusebius, "The Life of the Blessed Emperor Constantine," Book IV, Chap. XVIII, quoted in *A Select Library of Nicene and Post-Nicene Fathers of the Christian Church*, Vol. 1, Philip Schaff and Henry Ware, editors (New York: The Christian Literature Company, 1890), p. 545.

[63] *Ibid.*

[64] *Ibid.*, p. 544.

Saturday designated it as a festival and a day of worship. There is also a bulk of evidence in the works of Chrysostom and other writers in the fourth century that a service with epistle and gospel readings and a sermon was held on both days.

What, then, precipitated the famous edict of Constantine in 321? [65] That edict said: "All judges, city people and craftsmen shall rest on the venerable day of the Sun. But countrymen may without hindrance attend to agriculture, since it often happens that this is the most suitable day for sowing grain or planting vines, so that the opportunity afforded by divine providence may not be lost, for the right season is of short duration." [66] He also enjoined "all soldiers—pagan or otherwise to pray on an open plain near the city— and by a signal to offer a prayer which they had learned." [67] Constantine himself prescribed what the prayer should be: "We acknowledge thee the only God: we own thee as our King, and implore thy succor. . . . Together we pray to thee, and beseech thee long to preserve to us, safe and triumphant, our Emperor Constantine and his pious sons." [68]

Whether Constantine was a Christian in any sense of the word other than the political has never been ascertained. But that his edict of March, 321, and subsequent orders concerning Sunday were political, in spite of the fact that he may have been utterly sincere, is difficult to deny. He appealed both to the sun worshipers and

[65] András Alföldi in his *The Conversion of Constantine and Pagan Rome* (London: Oxford, 1948), p. 130, quotes in translation A. Piganiol's book *L'Empereur Constantin:* "Unfortunately we cannot date exactly Constantine's first law on the Sabbath rest. The text that we possess was posted up in Sardinia, in March or July A.D., 321, but a long interval often elapsed between the issue of an edict and its publication in the provinces. On the other hand, this text seems to be correcting an older law and softening its prescriptions. Constantine had ordered that the tribunals should be closed on the Sunday. Now he goes back on that order and decides that they shall remain open for enfranchisements and emancipations. He also decides to except the peasants from compulsory idleness, in order that they may be able to take advantage of the fine weather that Providence gives them. We incline to think that the first measures, taken by Constantine in relation to the Sunday rest, were earlier than A.D. 321. A curious text of an inscription from Pannonia, unfortunately not dated, C.I.L. iii 4121, tells us that in this province, Constantine fixed the Sunday as market day, perhaps in order to make it easier to break off hard work."

[66] Henry Bettenson, *Documents of the Christian Church,* Codex Justinianus, III, xii, 3 (New York: Oxford University Press, 1947), p. 27.

[67] Eusebius, *op. cit.,* Chap. XIX, p. 545.

[68] *Ibid.,* Chap. XX, p. 545.

to the Christ worshipers by ordaining Sunday as an official holy day. Pagans and Christians alike were to offer prayer, and the subject of the prayer was himself!

The Roman legions and the civil branches were so made up of worshipers of Mithras, "the Unconquerable Sun," who recognized Caesar as the medium of divine favor, that Constantine could well afford some appeasement as he transferred the official religion from his former faith of Mithraism to the new Christianity. Mithraism "had so much acceptance that it was able to impose on the Christian world its own Sun-day in place of the Sabbath, its Sun's birthday, 25th December, as the birthday of Jesus." [69]

There was no Christmas until the fourth century. "Christmas is not a spontaneous creation by the early, missionary kerygma. Almost two centuries before Christmas was celebrated, the church began to observe the festivals of the martyrs as persons. They proclaim death as the form of existence of the Body of Christ, the way in which the congregation follows its Head through the cross to the resurrection. . . . There is no indication that the birth and Christmas stood in the center." [70] The Church was concerned with the death and resurrection of Jesus. Constantine and his successors of the fourth century compromised the faith officially with certain aspects of the Sun's religion.

The fourth-century compromise is far more inauspicious than the mere blending of the symbolism of an old paganism with a new faith. The very fact that the religion of Jesus for the first time became the religion of the state now subjects it to an entirely new legalism. For in creating a new theocracy and new religious laws, Constantine turned to the theocracy from which the Christian faith had come. Christianity, as a religion of the state, needed to rationalize and to find an explanation for the new legalism of national Christianity. And there was one section of Jewish legalism that would not be controversial. It was the Ten Commandments. Since Christians still read and respected the Old Testament, it was not difficult for them to regard the Ten Commandments as an adjunct to the Christian

[69] Thomas G. Tucker *et al.*, *The History of Christianity in the Light of Modern Knowledge* (New York: Harcourt, Brace and Company, Inc., 1929), p. 74.
[70] Gustaf Wingren, *Theology in Conflict* (Philadelphia: Muhlenberg Press, 1958), p. 121.

faith. They forgot about the context in which the Commandments were given, that they were for a Jewish theocracy, not for a Christian church, or even a Christian theocracy. Thus 1,300 years before the Puritans began to tamper with the Sabbath and fuse it with Sunday to derive a Christian Sabbath, Constantine had done that for which the Puritans are often given credit. The church writings reflect the thought of the time. In the first chapter of the "Homily of the Seed," attributed to Athanasius of the fourth century, is the argument that Christ himself transferred the day of the Sabbath to the Lord's Day. A fiction was promulgated. With the fourth century, therefore, the blue laws had their inception, and not in the Act of Uniformity of Edward VI in 1551 requiring church attendance and business closing on Sunday or in the Puritan-inspired legislation of the seventeenth century.

The matter was nearly complete. Christians began with the Jewish Sabbath, faithfully attending on the worship in the Temple in Jerusalem. Also, they met daily, breaking bread and reading the Scriptures. Then the first day received some emphasis, especially in I Corinthians, where Paul recommends a collection to be taken upon a certain first day. There was at the beginning of the second century, possibly at the close of the first century, the linking of the first day with the term, the "Lord's Day." As to whether this was because of the fact that Jesus rose from the dead on that day, the early accounts are not explicit. "They kept the first day of the week—possibly although not certainly (and perhaps even improbably) in memory of the resurrection of Jesus." [71] But in A.D. 110 Ignatius makes this link. Then Justin Martyr in A.D. 150 refers to the Lord's Day as the Sun's day. Meanwhile daily rituals continue and fast days are retained and revised with special emphasis on Friday; Saturday continues as a holy day of worship, particularly in the East and Africa, while it becomes a fast day, or day of preparation in the West. Then Constantine's edict binds Christians and pagans alike to certain Sunday observances. Sabbath observance fades fast in the West (it hangs on for another thousand years in Abyssinia and Egypt, areas closer to the Palestinian influence and

---

[71] Kenneth Scott Latourette, A History of the Expansion of Christianity, Vol. I, "The First Five Centuries" (New York: Harper and Brothers, 1937), p. 305.

areas cut off several centuries later from the influence of the West by the Mohammedan invasion). With the functions of church and state now overlapping, a new legalism sets in with Sunday. An attempt is made to explain Sunday in terms of the Jewish Sabbath. And the Jewish Sabbath, which does not have to be on a Saturday according to certain Jewish authorities,[72] actually rotates for Christians and becomes reincarnated in all of its legalism on Sunday.

[72] Cf. Hirsch, *The Jewish Encyclopedia, op. cit.,* pp. 602, 603.

IV THE SHADOW OF AN EMPEROR

One is tempted to say that Sunday is a secular idea—that it belongs to a Roman emperor. But Constantine was more than an emperor. He was a protector of the faith, an establisher of religious ideas. Constantine was a symbol of a strange triune—Christianity, paganism, the civil authority.

When Constantine built his beautiful Constantinople along the Bosporus, he erected a statue of the Greek sun-god, Apollo, struck off the head and substituted a new head of himself. Inside the statue he placed a piece of wood supposedly from the holy cross. Constantine dipped into the Judaeo-Christian tradition and pagan sun worship for his ideas, and though he clothed them and sanctioned them with the authority of the state, they remained religious ideas.

Sixteen hundred years after Constantine enacted the first Sunday law, Sunday is still with us, hardly seriously challenged by any major group of the church. And with Sunday are other attributes of the age of Constantine.

Ever play charades? To play charades you usually need two teams —one team acts out a subject, the other guesses, then they switch around. Pretend that we are playing charades. Each side has been asked to depict a period in history, and some aspect of that period of history. Strangely enough both sides, though they choose separate centuries, decide to depict the role of the church in relationship to the state. Sounds like an "egghead" party, doesn't it? But play the game—by the way, see if you can guess the century that each group of actions is depicting.

GROUP I: An eleven-foot statue of the Virgin Mary, the largest that can be found, is erected on the steps of the Capitol building, for a rally in the name of the Virgin.

Freedom of speech and expression have limitations, a bishop says, and must be curtailed "in the interest of truth, decency and national security."

All coins are to be struck with words showing that the leaders trust in the God of the Judaeo-Christian tradition.

All religious vestments and "regalia" may be brought into the country from foreign principalities duty free.

The leader of the nation openly attends on Christian worship, encouraging others to do so.

Jews, while they are not required to attend Christian places of worship, shall be expected by economic coercion, fines, property confiscation to conform to the worship pattern of the majority national religion, which is that of Jesus Christ, and therefore keep holy the Christian day of worship.

Religious institutions may receive special endowment directly and indirectly from the government.

GROUP II: The leaders of the church shall receive richly adorned Bibles from the government.

A bishop praises the head of government and the close association of church and state as signs of God.

Coins are to be struck with symbols to show that the leaders trust in the God of the Judaeo-Christian tradition.

The leader of the nation asks for prayers to be said on his behalf.

The leader of the nation openly attends on Christian worship, and encourages others to do so.

Statues with religious subjects are erected in public places and in government buildings.

Jews, while they are not required to attend Christian worship, are required, if they live in the city, to refrain from work on Sunday.

Which one of the above sequences would you put in the fourth century, which one in the twentieth century in the United States?

There are similarities, are there not?

Where did you place Group I? It belongs in the United States, in the 1950's. The first incident mentioned was to occur on the steps of the state Capitol in St. Paul, Minnesota—the statue, a copy of the original in Lourdes, France, was to be brought in and placed on a 17-foot pedestal at the base of the Capitol steps, towering over the permanent statues of governmental leaders. The occasion was to be a Family Rosary Crusade rally, October 5, 1958. The quotation is from a Roman Catholic bishop before delegates of a Knights of Columbus convention discussing the necessity of laws against calumny, libel, and slander, and other matters such as salacious literature and matters of national security. Coins bear the official government motto "In God We Trust." (A new United States series of "American credo" religious stamps and a ten-cent airmail stamp with a Bible verse are planned for 1960.) The duty-free permit on religious articles was signed by President Eisenhower in August, 1958. He attends church. The reference to the Jews includes all seventh-day observers and, though harshly stated, is true in virtually all of the states in the Union (see Chapter I), in some affecting only seventh-day barbers, in others affecting all lines of work. And seminaries and church colleges benefit from tax exemption, long-range loans with low government interest, and government loans for Th.D. students under Title IV of the National Defense Education Act of 1958.

How about Group II? This group of actions, which took place at the time of Constantine in the fourth century, sounds strangely like the other series of events in Group I which took place in the United States. Constantine gave rich gifts to his bishops, including ornate gold Bibles. This could happen in the United States, but usually the inverse is true, the President accepts specially bound volumes donated by religious societies. The other statements are close parallels to events in the present-day United States.

In both Constantine's century and ours Sunday laws are the progeny of a church-state relationship, one supplying the ideas, one coalescing the ideas and providing the authority. And in each case there is a stepchild or out-of-place member of the community family, a minority, which is not the offspring of church-state unions in the Christian era but which is a carryover of a church-state union that had long been dead but left its progeny, and which provides embarrassment to the Christian authority. This source of embarrassment is the Jew.

The Jew has always been a thorn in the flesh to the Christian state. Emperor Justinian (527–565) in his *Constitutions* speaks of his own methods as compared with those of his predecessors, who had permitted the Jews at least to assemble on their own Sabbath. Under Justinian they were to be baptized, renounce their Sabbath and other rites, or suffer penalties which included death.

In 778 Pope Hadrian proclaimed Charlemagne to be a new type of Constantine through whom God would do many wonderful works. And on Christmas Day, 800, Pope Leo III "suddenly placed a precious crown on his head, and the dome resounded with the acclamations of the people, 'Long life and victory to Charles, the most pious Augustus, crowned by God, the great and pacific emperor of the Romans! . . .' His coronation oath represents a promise to maintain the faith and privileges of the church." [1]

Charlemagne forbade Sunday work on farms, which Constantine had allowed. Church councils wrangled over what should be prohibited next. In 1009, prohibitions included markets, fairs, hunting, and ordinary labor; in 1031, traveling that was not of necessity or for acts of mercy; in 1050, all work and all traveling. In 1221, attendance at the Sunday mass and sermon was made obligatory on all.

From the time of Constantine's victory at the Mulvian bridge in 312 to the storming of the Bastille in Paris in 1789, there is a long Jewish Dark Ages. Jews were forced to submit to church rites, to wear badges of their identity. One after another the nations of Europe were closed to them. For a long time Spain received Jews, but then a wave of massacres swept the peninsula. To save their lives many Jews were baptized, as they were in other areas. Those who were baptized but continued to hand along secretly their beliefs and traditions were called marranos. To get at these Jews an Inquisition was inaugurated in 1478. At last, in desperation over the problem of the crypto-Jew, Ferdinand and Isabella, in the same year that Columbus discovered America, issued an edict ordering all the Jews out of Spain. All Europe was closed to them except parts of Italy and Germany, and many remained in Spain to carry on their beliefs in complete secrecy. Only in 1959 was a Jewish synagogue opened in Spain, the first since 1492.

[1] Edward Gibbon, *The Decline and Fall of the Roman Empire* (New York: Random House, Inc., n.d.), Vol. III, Chap. 49, p. 33.

In England and its colonies the Jews were out of place. Sunday laws came to England with the coming of the missionary Augustine and the conversion of the Saxon kings. In colonial New England the Jews fled the Puritan colonies to the more hospitable Maryland, but found they could not wholly escape Sunday laws and other impositions of a unilateral religious influence. They did find refuge in Rhode Island where was established the first free synagogue in America.

Strangely enough, although most Jews will agree that the Hebrew people have had more freedom in modern America than in any period of the last twenty-six centuries (from the captivity to the present day), they are nevertheless still considerably out of place in American society. At first one is shocked to hear Paul Tillich say that anti-Jewish feeling is "stronger in the United States than it was in Germany before Hitler." He was answering questions in connection with a lecture series at the University of Chicago, in January, 1959.

A majority religion sponsored, or permitted authority for its views, by the state can never keep in mind the needs of small, radically different units. The body politic does not have the compassion of Christ. Even within the church sphere itself, the majority group does not have sufficient identity to have compassion for the individual. I saw this illustrated some years ago in Chicago. Everyone knows the compassion of the members of the Salvation Army. A big Salvation Army rally had just ended. Outside the building, on a park bench, sat a miserable-looking fellow, heavily inebriated. It was noontime, Sunday. Perhaps someone stopped to offer the fellow a sandwich, or to talk with him for a moment, but the hordes of Salvationists ahead of us paid no heed. Is this an allegory of the group, the result of a compromise of a composite of individuals? Somebody—the needy, the down and out—gets lost in the shuffle, even at a Salvation Army convention.

Thus it is important for the church to keep alive a certain commiseration for the Jews. For by being wholly concerned with the Jew, and with every minority within its society, the church can purge itself of the stigma of Constantine. Whether the church must be a minority, which it most assuredly becomes when it loses government sanctions, is an academic question. But most certainly the church must be separated from the state, whether the state is just or not, if the church is to be close to the heart of the minority and to the heart of its Savior. Apart from the state the church will at least be free from politican pagan influence. Admittedly the pagan or secular influence may be just. But the church actually is not. It is composed of members theoretically redeemed by grace. And when it functions as such a body, it remains within its legitimate sphere. But when the church approves an arrangement and suggests definite sectarian policies, receiving a blessing from the state in return, the church bestows its "holy" justice or "holy" injustice officially on its own, while the uninitiated loses the favor of the state.

To keep today's organized religion, Christianity, close to the personal, compassionate Christ, Tillich suggests paying particular attention to the role of the Jew. "One thing for Christians to remember is that the very existence of Judaism is a corrective against pagan danger," says Tillich. "That is important, because when Christianity becomes too much interwoven in the nation which accepts it, Christianity easily becomes pagan. I speak from my own life experience. My Jewish friends always showed me when my thinking was in danger of becoming paganized." [2] Dietrich Bonhoeffer had thoughts along the same line. "Only he who cries out for the Jews has the right to sing Gregorian chants," [3] he said. Whenever a church seeks to impose on other members of the society the religious content of its faith, no matter how it may clothe that content in terms of desirability, the church has resorted to tyranny and become a slave of pagan forces, religious or secular, that are contrary to the spirit of its Savior and Redeemer. "The seeds of Dachau are in every heart . . . in the hearts that beat beneath yellow skin, black skin, brown skin, white skin," said the Reverend Frank F. Drowata of Woodmont Christian Church, Nashville, at the 1959 International Convention of Christian Churches meeting in Denver. "Whenever a dislike for a minority group, whenever misunderstanding, or whenever prejudice grows into hate, it can grow into the final act . . . the murder of Dachau." The character of the compromise in which a church is engaged can be seen in the treatment of religious minorities, the nonmembers of that compromise.

[2] Paul Tillich, at the University of Chicago, Jan. 8, 1959.
[3] Quoted by Peter Berger, "Camus, Bonhoeffer, and the World Come of Age, II," in the *Christian Century*, April 15, 1959, p. 451.

In Russia [4] the Jews are beginning to have a hard time of it. And this is interesting, particularly in light of a general toleration of the Christian religion in Russia. Khrushchev, talking with Senator Hubert Humphrey of Minnesota, assured Humphrey that there was no persecution of Jews in Russia. Yet a Russian Jew in a recent interview with an American reporter indicated that although there is no open hostility against the Jews at present, on every hand there is developing anti-Semitism. Jews have been quietly eased out of all offices. An intense propaganda campaign blasting living conditions in Israel has been so effective that only a small handful of Jews sought to go to Israel in 1958. No Yiddish or Jewish publications are permitted in the USSR. Jews see each other at weekly Sabbath meetings, but there are no mass rallies or gatherings of rabbis. "Thus the 'thaw' in the USSR has given Jews less cause to rejoice than most other people. The situation of Soviet Jews has improved inasmuch as their active persecution has halted. But they are still the victims of discrimination. The Jewish religion is still among the least favored in the Soviet Union, and the opposition to most expressions of Jewish national life continues." [5] The Jews, then, are oppressed psychologically if not physically in a state where they are not on a par with the Orthodox Church, which exists in a theocratic compromise with the state. Says *Collier's Encyclopedia* concerning the Orthodox Church: "The church submitted without protest to the limitation of its powers, and showed its readiness to obey the government. Collaboration proved fruitful . . . national rest days were made to coincide with church holidays, and on September 4, 1943, the patriarchate was restored. In 1950 the status of the [Russian] church was that of an instrument of the Soviet State." [6]

Consider the status of the Jew in America. Is he oppressed? It is important that we face this question, if we are interested in finding

[4] There are no problems of Sunday-closing enforcement for a church in a society in which sanction comes from a state for a church idea. In the first place, there are no privately owned shops which Jews or others could keep open on Sunday; second, there are severe penalties from absence from Soviet businesses for religious services.

[5] Walter Laqueur, "Soviet Policy and Jewish Fate," in *Commentary*, October, 1956, p. 312.

[6] Oleg A. Maslenikov, "Union of Soviet Socialist Republics," under "Religion," in *Collier's Encyclopedia*, Vol. 19, Charles P. Barry, editor-in-chief (New York: P. F. Collier and Son, 1952), p. 37.

correctives for compromised religion, or rather religion receiving favor because of mutual arrangement with the state. Compromise in religion, as we have it, is not necessarily bad. That is another matter. But even a good thing, if we prefer to call it such, needs a corrective. This Tillich knows only too well, having lived in Nazi Germany and in the United States.

How does a Jew, or a member of another minority group, such as a Seventh-day Adventist or a Seventh-day Baptist, look at religion in the United States today? We shall not probe sociological matters, such as housing, employment, schools, ghettos. Let us take a matter related to our discussion, weekly worship, and in particular Sunday and Sunday laws as promulgated unilaterally by government and the great church bodies.

What does a Jew or Adventist see? Would the Sunday laws appear to be a boon, neutral, or a great danger? Would they appear beneficial, indifferent, or oppressive?

As our viewpoints shift to the minority, perhaps our judgments change. Following are questions raised by Jews and Adventists. The more rhetorical questions are left out. These appear to be the real questions:

1. *What determines the morality of an act?*

Is morality a concern of legislation? If so, how does a legislative body determine what is moral and what is not? Can the Congress or the state legislature decide what is moral?

The moral customs of some nations in the past and in the present have permitted polygamy. But not in the United States. Polygamy is considered, for our society, immoral, and thus also illegal. Morality depends on certain values. First of all, if health and welfare are considered top values by a government, the government is not likely to let that value be subservient to other values such as esthetics or religion. The government makes the value of health and welfare of infinite worth. Religion would place it on a lower scale and make it relative to other considerations: "I beseech you therefore, brethren, by the mercies of God, that ye present your bodies a living sacrifice. . . ."[7] There are other considerations, according to St. Paul. But the state makes health a primary value.

[7] Romans 12:1.

The state has a right to be concerned with the health of its people. Health, as a universally accepted value, is a moral subject. Thus the populace applauds when a child is given a tranfusion over the objections of his Jehovah's Witness parents or when a polygamous group is broken up in the West. These religious questions can be argued as moral in our society.

To be moral, as long as we choose to talk in terms of morality, the requirement must be applicable to all men, a self-evident premise that, although it may be incapable of being proved, is incapable of being disproved. The moral act will be that indicated in Kant's categorical imperative: "There is therefore but one categorical imperative, namely this: *Act only on that maxim whereby thou canst at the same time will that it should become a universal law.*" [8] The Golden Rule says the same thing: "Whatsoever ye would that men should do to you, do ye even so to them." [9] Now what determines whether an action on Sunday is good or bad, moral or immoral? The state cannot do so, for it is dealing with religious terms that have long been defined as religious ideas. The state has authority, but to know how to legislate, it must turn to the church. The state takes its cue from the church in regard to Sunday, directly or indirectly.

Can the state legislate in the matters of days? To do so it must be able to determine that Sunday inactivity is a matter of health. But who is to say that Sunday work is bad? I know a minister who works like a fiend on Sunday—preaches two radio services in the morning, then conducts a midnight radio service in the evening. His act is not immoral. He gets another day off, a month's vacation. What makes this arrangement moral for him and immoral for someone else, such as a Jewish merchant? The gist of the matter is that the state is attempting to determine what is moral in a sphere in which it has no criteria for deciding what is moral. There is no common basis for decision. For how can a state say that rest on a certain day is more moral than rest on another day, or even for that matter that one twenty-four-hour day is normative and moral for all men? The state regards these as moral decisions; yet it has no grounds for doing so except the coercion of the church and a set of principles that orig-

[8] Immanuel Kant, "Transition from Popular Moral Philosophy to the Metaphysic of Morals," in *The Harvard Classics*, Charles W. Eliot, editor (New York: P. F. Collier and Son, 1910), pp. 351, 353.

[9] Matthew 7:12.

inate with the church. Sunday or Saturday observance is not a moral question, but the state makes it so, and thus, through the sanctions of a theocratic relationship, can say that what is good on one day is bad on another and, conversely, that what is bad on Sunday is acceptable on Monday.

Consider this statement from the United Church of Canada: "The point to note is that none of these things (motoring, skiing, skating, golfing), as such, is harmful. In fact, the very opposite can be said of most of these activities; that is, they are good. But when they take primacy over the religious and restful purpose of the Lord's Day they become subversive to the highest interests of man." [10] A Jew would invert this concept of morality. He would complain that the Lord's Day has become subversive to the highest interests of man (and these could include, even on his own Sabbath, motoring, skiing, golfing, and the like as long as they did not interfere with his thirty-nine restrictions of the Talmud). Which is right—a theocratic Christian view or a more liberal view? It would depend on whether morality is seen in the shadow of Constantine or in terms of more inalienable categories such as the welfare of *all* men.

2. *What does Sunday promulgated by state authority actually do to one of Sunday's intended goals, the achievement of a family rest day?*

Assuredly, the blue laws exist in the present day, not so much for the achievement of a Jewish literalism in Christianity, as was the case in Puritanical New England, but for the purpose of keeping the family together, and to call attention of the family to its spiritual needs. Pope Pius XII put it this way as he was speaking to a quarter of a million members of Italian Catholic Action in St. Peter's Square in 1947: "Sunday must become again the day of the Lord, the day of adoration, of glorification and reflection, the day of happy reunion in the intimate circle of the family." Granted that worship and family reunion are worthy goals. But they raise two questions for the Jew, as they should also for the Christian: (1) Should these goals be primary or secondary in the life under God, and (2) do the blue laws help to achieve them?

[10] "Why Sunday?" excerpts from the report of the Commission on the Lord's Day, given "general approval" by the Thirteenth General Council of the United Church of Canada, Vancouver, 1948, issued by the Board of Evangelism and Social Service, UCC, Toronto, p. 21.

Governor Frank Clement, in Tennessee, in pardoning a Baptist minister cited for contempt of court for refusing to divulge information received in a divorce case, declared, "There is nothing more important to us than our homes, and we must do everything we can to let husbands and wives in distress know they can go to their spiritual advisors for counseling." A man's home and family are no doubt the dearest thing to him—particularly in the United States. But is his home the most important thing? Dr. Ellis A. Fuller, the late president of Southern Baptist Theological Seminary, once said to his students: "When I proposed to my wife I offered her second place in my heart —Christ will always be first." In the Hebrew Scriptures, the family clearly is not the most important aspect of a person's existence. From Genesis to Job to Amos to Malachi, God is foremost, man and his family second, in importance. Abraham placed God first, even to the point of being willing to sacrifice his son, Isaac; Job suffered the loss of all he had, his possessions, his family, in the test to see which he placed first, God or his family; Amos and the prophets through Malachi berated the Israelites for putting God last, Amos because they built summer homes and drank so much wine they could drink it out of bowls, Malachi because they spent too much money on the everyday things of life, failing to do without on an individual and family level in order to bring greater and better sacrifices into the House of God. In the Hebrew Commandments there are commandments that encourage a happy family life, factors that are important in religious existence, or rather perhaps as a by-product of religious existence, such as honoring a person's father and mother, keeping the sanctity of the marriage vows, watching a person's use of language, taking care not to kill or covet, all of which have direct bearing on the home, particularly in relationship to the Creator. Yet God for the Hebrew is central—thus the first two commandments start with God, and with the admonition that there is to be no other god or any graven image before or in substitute for God. Read the sixth chapter of Deuteronomy. There is no doubt what is the most important facet of the Jewish life. "Hear, O Israel: The Lord our God is one Lord: And thou shalt love the Lord thy God with all thine heart, and with all thy soul, and with all thy might. And these words, which I command thee this day, shall be in thine heart: And thou shalt teach them diligently unto thy children, and shalt talk of them when thou sittest in thine house, and when thou walkest by the way, and when thou liest down, and when thou risest up." [11] Jesus also repeats the heart of this chapter, the *shema yisrael,* "Hear, O Israel," that the Lord God is one, indivisible, totally demanding in life, and totally involved to the point of His giving His all, even His only begotten Son. Jesus knows what it means to love God with all his heart, soul, strength. He saw his mother heartbroken beneath the cross. He warned his followers that those who follow Him must bear a cross, a cross that might go against the grain of family life,[12] that could split family ties.[13] The religion of the Jews and the religion of Jesus can consummate home life and they can wreck it totally. The fact that Sunday must be kept aside as a holy day in homage to God is in itself a terrible thought for a Christian in an ethic of involvement. But more terrible is the naïve popular assumption that Sunday must be preserved as a day for the family's moral and spiritual benefit. Observing a family day on a day also set aside for God, and defending the institution on the basis of family necessity, appear to be not only irreligious but blasphemy.

If Sunday could be demonstrated as necessary for upholding family life, then the question would follow whether blue laws achieve this purpose. What do blue laws do for the family on Sunday: They are wholly negative—they tell a family and their neighbors what they cannot do. This negativism in a progressive society is a question to consider in itself. Have you ever worked with young people, with your own children? You have to say "No" many times, but you also find that saying "Don't, don't, don't," over and over again, deadens the response. You wonder why Johnny never hears you. You wonder why young people leave the church as soon as they are old enough to break away. It is a part of their physiology, their psychology. But perhaps it is also the reaction to an overdose of negativism in religion. Do the Sunday prohibitions of "Don't, don't, don't" keep children out of trouble? Or do these Sunday laws stagnate the day and open up other avenues of thrills, such as drag races, behind-the-barn activities, the parked cars at night overlooking the city that gives itself, in the name of religion, a shot of morphine on a day in which nothing constructive or creative is scheduled for young people?

[11] Deuteronomy 6:4–7.
[12] Luke 9:57–62.
[13] Matthew 10:34.

There is a current song which describes the lazy, nostalgic Sunday and the attraction it has for lovers with nothing very much to do except to be with each other. Is this the American Sunday, a sentimental Sunday with perhaps more roots in a Hollywood mentality of reminiscence than in a creative evangelical tradition? Anglican Bishop Henry Wolfe Baines of Singapore has an intelligent approach to Sunday that takes in more realistically the needs of the family on Sunday in the Space Age. He stirred religious circles by advocating Sunday volunteer work to help improve public recreation facilities. "Here is a chance to do good on the Sabbath," he wrote in the Selangor State parish magazine. "A new opportunity has been given for service in Singapore." Bishop Baines was referring to an appeal by the State of Singapore's minister of national development for volunteers to undertake tasks of "public social usefulness." The prelate added that clergy should schedule services at suitable times for the Sunday Voluntary Corps members, as is normally done for those who must work on the weekly holy day. Leaders of other denominations, however, and even some Anglicans, felt otherwise. Roman Catholic parishioners have been advised by clergy not to volunteer for the Sunday activities if manual labor were involved.

Laws, which are necessary, complicate life, but their complications also preserve order. For instance, where would we be without traffic laws? Restrictions preserve order. But restrictions on subjects outside the sphere of the state's concern on a religious subject such as preserving a holy day, and a special type of one at that, create more disorder than order. In the old Jewish theocracy, the Jewish restrictions, constantly divided and redivided and redefined to permit exceptions, caused more handicaps than existed without the exceptions. So it is with our pharisaical religious Sunday laws. The controversial Massachusetts law has had seventy amendments to it, and the Pennsylvania statute has accrued many exceptions, especially since the raising of fines. The problems the Sunday laws create for the family are many. In the first place, they are so anachronistic they cannot be enforced. This is openly admitted by almost every attorney general in the United States and Canada, and thus to wink at the law cannot help but encourage lawlessness. Second, they seek to negate certain Sunday family activities, such as Sunday driving, sports, boating, fishing, golf, picnics. By negation wholesome activities are discouraged; and by defining what is right and what is not right in the sphere of Sunday activity, the state unintentionally puts its stamp of approval on subversive, obscene, and perverted entertainments. It is impossible for a modern state to define its recreation entirely by law. When it says "no" to the obvious Sunday activities, such as bowling, golf, or Sunday movies, as many localities have done in Ontario recently by referendum, it opens the door for the illegitimate or less constructive activities. Thus in Port Dover, Ontario, it was possible in the 1950's to go to peep shows and penny arcades, and the like, on Sunday, but not to play golf or bowl on Sunday. The Maryland Court of Appeals upheld a conviction of a salesman who sold a toy submarine on Sunday, while the same blue law permits sale of liquor on Sunday, a situation which the trial judge himself vehemently deplored. Do blue laws preserve a family day? No, they deteriorate the day, as they would any day with the same restrictions. A definitive morality for the benefit of religion in the name of the family not only blasphemes God but threatens constructive family life, courts delinquency, and corrupts a respect for the law in a community.

3. *What do Sunday laws do to the guarantees and safeguards of the Constitution?*

The Constitution guarantees an individual freedom to act and to compete in the field of religion without coercion or restraints on his faith. Yet the Constitution is not clear in saying what these rights mean in practice and whether these rights which are guaranteed on a national level are also guaranteed on the state level. For example, it had been assumed for many years that all people were equal under the law of the land, but in regard to the racial question this had been construed to be "separate but equal" until the Supreme Court finally ruled that separate facilities were not equal. Concerning blue laws, the Federal Court has refused in the past to act concerning Sunday activity, leaving this action up to the states. The First Amendment says that "Congress shall make no law respecting an establishment of religion, or prohibiting the free exercise thereof. . . ." But this has been construed to apply to Congress only. The states could conceivably, by the right of state legislatures, make a law in a category that Congress would not. This conflict was partially corrected after the Civil War with the Fourteenth Amendment, which says that "no State shall make or enforce any law which shall abridge the privileges or immunities of citizens of the United States." This corrects the situation to a certain extent, but it does not bring the same limitation of the First Amendment on Congress to apply to the state legislatures.

Meanwhile, the states do what they wish in regard to Sunday regulations, and often, with old laws which predate the Constitution itself, attempt to decide what is right and wrong on Sunday. It is always questionable whether these laws are in keeping with the spirit of the Constitution.

The blue laws, as they are applied on the local scene, call into question the guarantees of the Constitution on many counts. But most obvious are these transgressions against the implicit guarantees of the First and Fourteenth amendments:

Sunday laws are confiscatory.

Actually all laws are confiscatory to some degree. Repeated violations mean successive increases in the stringency of the penalty. Repeated fines can mean loss of property. Property can be a broad term. Madison included one's time and religion in "property rights." [14] A delicatessen owner's time is closely related to his property—if he is not allowed to keep long hours he is forced out of business. Says the late Frank H. Yost, former editor of *Liberty* magazine, referring to recent legislation proposed in Massachusetts: "We do not need a recession to kill off the small businessman—just a lot of Sunday laws." [15]

Blue laws can force confiscation of a person's religion, or at least ask for confiscation of his religion, if a job is accepted or continued when one's religion is opposed to the requirements of a job. Recently a guard at Riker's Island penitentiary, New York, became a Seventh-day Adventist and lost his job when he refused to continue working on Saturday. Strangely enough, back in high school the author quit a Woolworth dime-store job because the management wanted him to take inventory on Sunday morning—he said he would work on Christmas day, the following Tuesday, but not on Sunday, so he quit and went to work next door at the grocery store. It was the privilege

---

[14] *Cf.* Gaillard Hunt, editor, *Writings of James Madison* (New York: G. P. Putnam's Sons, 1906), Vol. 6, pp. 101–103.

[15] Frank H. Yost, "Would You Believe It?" *Library*, Fourth Quarter, 1958, p. 31.

of management to determine the working days. What becomes confiscatory is the action of government in forcing a holy day on a religion which does not observe that holy day; the competition becomes unfair, and possibly disastrous. The question of property rights has come up in several states. Around 1930 the Kentucky Supreme Court ruled that the owner of a theater had "no property rights which involved seven-day business." In 1889 a Mr. King, a Seventh-day Adventist, was arrested in Tennessee for plowing on Sunday. Said the justice in charge in refusing to grant a new trial: "The law is clear. I charged it properly. The fine is a reasonable one, and one well warranted. The laws are made to be obeyed; and Mr. King and all other men should and must obey them, or leave the country. I make these remarks that they may know that I intend to have the laws strictly enforced in the future." [16] The Supreme Court of Tennessee two years later upheld the verdict. The defendant's eventual alternative, the judge suggested, if he persisted in breaking the law, would be to leave the country.

Sunday laws are discriminatory.

On November 7, 1956, a thirty-six-year-old New York photographer was found guilty of violation of the Sabbath law for painting his mother-in-law's house on Sunday. How many people do you know who have done some painting on Sunday in reference to decorating, interior or exterior? I know some very fine church leaders in my community who have not only given many hours on Sunday to the church but who also, because of a heavy schedule during the week, painted on Sunday. I remember one of the most active deacons and Sunday-school teachers at the North Shore Baptist Church, Chicago. One Sunday he did not get to church. The following Sunday I asked where he had been, and he explained quite honestly that he had been laying tile the Sunday before. Now I do not recommend laying tile on Sunday, nor do I recommend that an individual who does so be haled into court for it. Millions decorate their homes on Sunday. Whether this is good or bad, whether it is of the devil or not, is beside the point. The fact is that a very few are penalized, while thousands and millions escape penalty. In New York in September, 1959, a young man who repaired his sports car on Sunday, was haled into

[16] Quoted in *American State Papers*, William Addison Blakely, editor (Washington: The Religious Library Association, 1949), p. 491.

court for working on Sunday. In Little Rock, as we have seen, and in the similar Berlon Taylor case at the Jefferson County seat of Pine Bluff to the southeast of Little Rock, the grocers haled into court are always the same ones, while admittedly from testimony quoted earlier we saw that others were open on Sunday.

Blue laws discriminate against products, favoring beer and prohibiting milk, or favoring the soft-drink dispenser while prohibiting both beer and milk sales. In Massachusetts it is illegal to dig for clams on Sunday but not to dredge for oysters or dig ditches. The law permits bakeries to stay open but not certain delicatessens. Opera is prohibited in the State of Pennsylvania on Sunday, but not football or baseball. Soccer is allowed, but not hockey.

Blue laws discriminate against religion. Rather, they discriminate against the minority religion. It would be a shocking thing if the government required an across-the-board observance of one of the Hebrew laws or customs. Take the Sabbath, Saturday. If the legislatures should write laws on the books that there would be no work on Saturday except that of necessity but that it would be acceptable to work on Sunday there would be a terrific commotion. The Christian religion is the one that seeks to be preserved by the laws. This cannot help but appear discriminatory to the non-Christian.

Sunday laws make the innocent criminal.

The attempt in New Jersey, and other states, has been to get away from the stigma of criminality which the Sunday laws often carry with them when they are administered under the criminal section of a law. The tendency is to transfer the legislation concerning a holy day to a disorderly-persons section of the law. Nevertheless, when a person is arrested, no matter under what part of the law he is called in question, it mars his record. An alien risks deportation. A Sunday violator convicted in Canada risks his whole future, if he should want to go to the United States, for that country has the right to deny entry to any individual convicted of a crime.

This startling fact was proved recently when a New Westminster police commissioner was hauled into court for being absent from church because his wife was ill. The charge was laid by a newspaper reporter to demonstrate how outmoded Lord's Day legislation really is. This case, which at first inspired many an amused smile, turned out to be not so funny when it was learned that the charge came under criminal law and, as such, had serious implications, possibly barring the commissioner from entry into the United States and in other ways placing a mark on a fine service record. The charge was laid aside, but only after it had been thoroughly established that the statute was still in effect, and that anyone who does "unlawfully fail to exercise himself in the duties of piety and true religion publicly and privately," is liable to a fine, upon conviction of five shillings, or 75 cents.[17]

Employees of stores arrested for Sunday work, as they have been by the droves in the Two Guys From Harrison stores, acquire a record. Thus a person can become a criminal, when he chooses for one reason or another to affront the popular religious mentality and violate the state-sanctioned holy day.

To the minority objector, in spite of the opinion that the majority must rule and in so doing impose its prejudices and special, precise religious beliefs on a minority, Sunday legislation, in its reasoning and in its content, looks strangely like a medieval inquisition, modified in time and place and in association with some liberal ideals inherent within our democracy. As minorities point out the blemishes on a democratic system, the eyes that should see them are dulled by a shadow that has plagued the visible church in society since the days of Constantine. The Constitution, particularly in the first Ten Amendments, has tried to guarantee equal rights for all, but the blight of oppression still clings to the state statutes, a fading blight in regard to segregation, but a blight that is still very active in the Sunday laws.

4. *What effect do the Sunday laws have on a plural society?*

When the Christian religion is confused with American patriotism and certain democratic ideals, then the self-exalted patriot argues that what is good for the Christian religion is good for the country, even such restrictive, discriminatory legislation as the Sunday laws. But when a person lifts his sights and realizes that God is greater than any one nation and that religion that is confused with patriotism is in the long run a false one, and the national God a false god, then one realizes that a plural, competitive, balanced society, with a maxi-

---

[17] The Rev. John G. Ferry, pastor of St. John's United Church, Vancouver, "The Lord's Day Act: Safeguard or Roadblock," Toronto *Star Weekly*, May 3, 1958.

mum of freedom and a minimum of limitations, has roots deeper than restrictive prejudicial legislation.

Aldous Huxley's *Brave New World* and George Orwell's *1984* describe the anonymity of life where there is mass organization under one principle of authority. Already the Chinese communes loom as the perfect antithesis of plural society. The American and Canadian shudder at that regimented type of life. Personality needs to be preserved; differences of opinions should be enhanced, not stunted. Yet strangely enough we tend to move in directions of monopolies of opinions, though we retain a general structure that permits a wide diversity of opinion. Paul Martin, writing an editorial in the Lansing, Michigan, *State Journal,* pleaded with the citizens to oppose a comprehensive Sunday-closing bill and thus take a decisive step to preserve a diversity of opinion. "One of the sources of this country's greatness is the opportunity for diversity of public opinion." Millions go to church, he said. "Many do not go to church. Some spend the Sabbath at home. Some play golf or go to the movies. Others operate businesses in order to make a living. Others become employees of such businesses for the same reason. Some Americans do not patronize business places on Sunday. Others do." There is a sizable minority that believes that a holy day should be Saturday instead of Sunday. Says Mr. Martin: "If the foundations of free America are to remain strong in the face of the threat posed by governments which depend for their power on rigid regimentation of the people, freedom of choice must continue to be safeguarded against limitations which are not clearly in the public interest." [18]

The minorities, though they may exaggerate the situation, look at the Sunday laws with dread, with an eye not merely on their present situation, but on the implications of such legislation to society. It is possible that eventually the genius of America and Canada will break down these laws, as we saw in Chapter I. But in the meantime, the longer the church remains silent or on the side of the blue laws, the more the church will suffer, the more Western society will suffer, and possibly, since time for effective adaptation to the Space Age may be short, anachronisms such as Constantine's church-state ar-

[18] Feb. 19, 1958.

rangement and Sunday restrictive laws could greatly affect the creative role of Western society.

5. *Who benefits from the Sunday laws?*

Laws bring prestige to the administrative bodies and also to those who initiate and sanction the laws. The Comintern in Russia makes its unilateral laws and decrees. Although the satellites have no part in the decisions, by endorsing and agreeing to the decisions they receive the prestige and authority along with those who initiated the ideas. And the Western church, initiating and lobbying for Sunday laws, though it has no authority, concurs with the authoritative bodies launching those laws. A power church is established. American Protestantism, though seemingly pluralistic in organization, is strongly cohesive in specific areas. It agrees on certain matters and has ambitions that compare in ideas, and almost in enthusiasm, with the Roman Catholic Church. "American Protestantism has behaved like a sect armed with the world power of a church," says William Lee Miller of the Yale Divinity School.[19]

As one person has said recently, it was God in the Jewish times who hallowed the Sabbath, but now it is the corner policeman, for the corner policeman becomes an active cohort of the Christian ministry, probably performing more directly for the church in general than many deacons and elders do for their local congregations. A near riot occurred last summer in Bristol Borough near Philadelphia when a dozen policemen raided a Bristol County supermarket and hauled thirty-five employees away in school buses to the borough hall, obliging them to post bail for a hearing.

Consider police action in Cincinnati. Cincinnati newspaper files are full of Police Chief Stanley Schrotel's slashing crusades against pinball machines, obscene literature, and other vices. An upstanding individual, with a class of sophomore boys in the suburban Westwood Presbyterian Church, Schrotel is also a deacon in that church. Recently he added one more crusade to his list: enforcement of Sunday laws. And when Schrotel does anything he does it well, that is, as far as it is possible. That is a reason he was considered as a possibility to head Chicago's police force following the 1960 Chicago police scandals. Yet one can never enforce blue laws well, especially the out-

[19] William Lee Miller, "Religion and the American Way of Life" in *Religion and the Free Society* (New York: Fund for the Republic, 1958), p. 19.

dated Ohio laws, for if a person did he would be locking up everybody. At the time Schrotel began his crackdown, nearly the entire city council, mayor and all, were leading churchmen. And the persistent arrests which followed were an indication of someone's religion, not one person, but a group mentality, supported by the religious constituency of the city. "Really," groaned one letter writer to a columnist in the Cincinnati *Post*, "is it up to the police and laws to enforce the rules of any religion in the United States, whether Christian, Jewish, or Moslem? . . . I myself love Sunday as my day of rest. I play golf on bright Sunday afternoons. I hope the police won't go on from Sunday grocery stores to stop us from playing golf on Sunday." [20] The police did not go on—they had all they could do with the grocery business, but they do have assurance now from the recent refusal of the United States Supreme Court to consider the Coleman Ullman, Hamilton, and William Kidd, Cincinnati, cases, thus upholding the conviction of grocers. In October, 1959, Governor Michael V. Di Salle signed into law a measure which removed some of the 130-year-old restrictions on Sunday labor in Ohio. A person is now allowed to open concession stands at state and county fairs on Sundays, to travel and to witness sports events and other entertainment. Still outlawed are unnecessary businesses, employment of common labor, and selling liquor.

The implications of identifying certain religious ideas with the authority of the state are far reaching. Theologian Rudolf Bultmann says, "The consequence of such identification would be that people who feel bound to practice a 'Christian' politics will label 'un-Christian' those whose political convictions differ." [21]

Inquisition, with all the ugly characteristics of a medieval fiat, but without the same modes of enforcement, is the instrument of Sunday laws. This is as Jefferson predicted. Although an idealist, he was also realistic. He knew what happens to ideals. Thus he fought for the inclusion of every safeguard possible for the protection of the church and state from each other. He said:

The spirit of the times may alter, will alter. Our rulers will become corrupt, our people careless. A single zealot may commence persecuter, and

[20] Cincinnatus (Alfred Segal), Cincinnati *Post*, Oct. 18, 1956.
[21] Rudolf Bultmann, "Theology for Freedom and Responsibility," *Christian Century*, Aug. 27, 1958, p. 969.

better men be his victims. . . . From the conclusion of this war we shall be going down hill. It will not then be necessary to resort every moment to the people for support. They will be forgotten, therefore, and their rights disregarded. They will forget themselves, but in the sole faculty of making money, and will never think of uniting to effect a due respect for their rights. The shackles, therefore, which shall not be knocked off at the conclusion of this war, will remain on us long, will be made heavier and heavier, till our rights shall revive or expire in a convulsion.[22]

God save us from this convulsion, risking expiration, in an age when the alternative that looms the largest is Communist tyranny.

Constantine is still with us. His legacy is a fusion of certain Christian ideals with the authority of the state. Sunday laws began with Constantine. What can the church and the Christian individual say about the ominous shadow of a fourth century emperor over the free and equal exercise of religion in the United States and Canada? As a motion-picture projector constantly projects different pictures on a screen, so can the church project ideas on the secular screen other than those static ideas that are incubative for tyranny and inquisition.

Compromise is necessary for constructive action; for progress to be made in industry and national policies there must be some compromise. But compromise is shaped by the parties involved. The Jewish-Gentile compromise at the Jerusalem council kept features of both the Gentile and Jewish Christians. Roman Catholic concordats between church and state, Protestant church mergers, ecumenical meetings, and so on, keep features of the participating parties. The church, when it is a chief proponent in a compromise or combination of principles with the state, directly or indirectly, shapes the character of that compromise. Thus the responsibility of the church of Jesus Christ is tremendous—especially in determining the tone of compromise in societies that tend to be "Christian" democracies. The responsibility of alleviating the blue-laws controversies rests first with the church.

[22] Thomas Jefferson, "Notes on Virginia," Query XVII, *The Works of Thomas Jefferson*, Paul Leicester Ford, editor (New York: G. P. Putnam's Sons, 1904), Vol. 4, pp. 81, 82.

V ALTERNATIVES TO AN AMERICAN INQUISITION

In suggesting definite actions for the church, the alternatives to promoting Sunday-closing laws divide into two categories: first, that which is general, in the realm of theory and thought; second, that which individuals might do. There are a group category and an individual category. The two divisions are not exclusive—a church body might act on a local, specific scale; individuals or local groups might take the course of general, nonobjective action. Normally large groups cannot be specific, because their power to act, as well as their action, is a compromise of many divergent views (which they must consider if they are to speak at all as a democratic body). And, conversely, individuals, and even local congregations, do not possess the anonymity of the larger concerns, and in exercising their democratic prerogatives can speak more precisely.

WHAT THE CHURCH CAN DO

How can the church in the 1960's, finding itself in a compromised society, act in a "Christian democracy"? As the church realizes that it must compromise to some extent with state authority and also that compromise, because it sacrifices and loses something of the Spirit, is not the most desirable course, a basic plan of action opens up. The church will want to minimize compromise.

This makes sense. Any big corporation—and the organized church is no exception—is eager to forge ahead of its competitors, to free itself from that which holds it back. Compromise may ensure temporary security and gains. But it is the fresh approach that makes the greatest impact. In collective bargaining, in arbitration of any kind, in planning new products, there is a search for alternatives that will resolve stalemates and open up entirely new pursuits.

For creative spiritual action, there are these suggestions for the corporate church:

1. *Encourage novelty in its polity and statements.*

The word "novelty" is so strange to us it almost needs defining. It is the element of change, newness, unpredictability. The church must have this. It is the way of the Spirit. As compromise tends to weaken and cause the life and witness of the church to grow stale, efforts at novelty can serve to open new avenues for the church and also serve as a preventative for permanently taking any compromise seriously. Novelty in religion asks that everything constantly come under new appraisal, to be rejudged, reconsidered. "Stand fast therefore in the liberty wherewith Christ hath made us free, and be not entangled again with the yoke of bondage," [1] Paul said. Stand fast against the correlating forces; do not give in. When the doctors of the church encompass you, take a stand that is your own.

Now, this sounds strangely like individual action; it of course can be. But here is a course of action calling for the church, for the denomination to assert itself, not to rest on current trends of seeking common ground with a sister-type of denomination. Unity has its place, but unity is also a stagnant idea. In willing to be a political power the church thinks it needs to be unified or to appear as such. Assuredly, to be a political power the church needs to become one voice. But does the church need to be a political power? This tendency to misunderstand its responsibility in the world comes from Constantine, not Christ. The church in the American society would do better to assert its individualities rather than its unities, denominationalism rather than ecumenical proclivities.

In a classroom there is no real unity, except that which the teacher, the time, the walls contain. Each youngster is an individual; so is the church, and so are its individual members. The importance, the personality, the significance and power of each one is not realized

[1] Galatians 5:1.

until released into society; and as adults, in separate categories, constantly new categories, the individuals take new, effective roots. Let us not hold back or deaden the church by encouraging unnecessary compromises or compromises that can reap only numerical and political advantages. We should recognize, with Gustaf Wingren, that "the *kerygma* (the message of the Gospel) itself must therefore assume different forms, and change becomes the necessary mark of the correct interpretation of the biblical word." [2]

Compromise diminishes when the church introduces new alternatives. In respect to the blue laws, the church will want to look askance at the current temptations and make up its mind anew in consideration of all possibilities. In seeking to restore novelty, the church will want to pay attention to the bodies outside its own fellowship and outside the general social current, the minorities. There is no better place to seek and to encourage novelty than in the direction of the minorities. "The Christian cannot be on the side of the orders that set up the crosses of history. His place is with the victim—and with the rebel." [3]

2. *Be on guard against the stagnation of ideas.*

As the church introduces novelty into its life, it needs to be on guard against letting any new ideas jell into a permanent mold. The church needs constantly to redefine its structure. That is an advantage of the ecumenical movement. It challenges the churches to rethink their position in a modern age; furthermore, cooperative action permits the sharing of new and workable ideas. While there are these advantages, ecumenical thinking also brings more organization, and the problem of overorganization. I remember a comedy at one of the Chicago theaters about ten years ago. The name of the play was Two Blind Mice, and the subject was a lost bureau in Washington, supposedly originated long ago by a United States President but maintained now by two old ladies, a bureau retained, but out of place over the years. The church, like a secular government, needs to reactivate its bureaus, or dissolve them in favor of new groupings. Church groups, such as the WCTU, church boards, and the one-day-in-seven groups, such as the Lord's Day Alliance, should reevaluate the cir-

[2] Gustaf Wingren, *Theology in Conflict,* p. 105.
[3] Peter L. Berger, "Camus, Bonhoeffer, and the World Come of Age—II," *Christian Century,* April 15, 1959, p. 451.

cumstances and, though they may not want to change their basic ideas, at least bring their thinking into harmony with the times.

Church groups should observe a jubilee type of year, as the early Hebrews theoretically did every fifty years. In the Hebrew jubilee year, everything would be rearranged, even property rights. Now, if the Lord's Day Alliance, which is in its second century, should completely dissolve itself, retain its funds under new trusteeship representing laymen and young people in the new era, then hire a new staff, set new goals, and play its part in tune with the times, what an effective, positive organization it would become for the kingdom of God. The society might even take on a new name, for which there would be many alternatives, depending on the purposes and goals reestablished (some premises we suggest in the last two chapters). In the summer of 1959, the Lutheran Church-Missouri Synod, which doubled its membership in the past twenty-five years, moved to San Francisco to bring its machinery up to date. Changes in the synod's administrative structure were approved at its triennial convention. They had been recommended by a thirteen-member survey, a "Little Hoover" commission which had studied the synod's operations for the past three years. Establishment of an office of executive director, regrouping of the synod's present staff into three major administrative units, and formation of a council of administrators as the major coordinating agency of the synod were main features of the revamping. A fresh outlook and an ability constantly to reorganize are necessary in the Space Age.

Dr. Robert Boyd Munger, of First Presbyterian Church, Berkeley, California, has a policy of changing all organizations in his church as soon as they reach the stage of "running smoothly" and apparently effortlessly. He maintains that when they begin to run smoothly, they have reached the peak of effectiveness and from then on begin to lose. So in his church the effective group is dissolved, and a new organization or organizations are born. "The church has amazing vitality!" says one person who attends that church. The main thing is that church groups—local or national—should not be allowed to stagnate. Let us have some "jubilee" time within the church each year. Ideally, if this could be done with the staid denominations, if they could be dissolved (not merged), and a new series of regroupings made, the church would be much healthier. This, of course, is impossible. A culture cannot give up its past. Yet, with progressive leadership within a single organization, say, a denomination or an organization like the Lord's Day Alliance, a jubilee year—not a mere rededication, but an opportunity to rebuild with the tools and ideas of a new age, with the interposition of the personality of an unchanging Christ—could be declared.

3. *Avoid unilateral action.*

Further to minimize compromise, which begets one-sided legislation, the church will want to avoid group action, the unanimous voice resulting from compromise.

A church should never speak unanimously. It is best that it issue no report at all if it has to do so unanimously. If a church body feels it has something that must be said, whether significantly controversial or not, let it follow the procedure of the courts and issue a minority statement along with the majority opinion. If there is no minority opinion, let the church refrain from speaking, for there is then something terribly wrong and no report should be issued at all.

In regard to Sunday laws, then, where there is temptation to compromise internally so that one political voice can be presented, let the church bodies consider these alternatives in order to be a constructive spiritual force rather than a political lobby: (1) avoid statements on political issues altogether; (2) if the church must speak to a specific issue, let the church present a minority report along with the majority report; (3) let the church speak only to the spiritual factors involved and not to the specific political situation.

Some people would fear that the first and last alternative would make the church irrelevant, and that not to speak to an issue is not to speak to any at all. But this is the best way for the church to avoid becoming irrelevant. For instance, when the church pats the government on the back, so to speak, for its cooperation, or when, as in Russia and the United States, the church gives direct sanction to political maneuvers, it then becomes irrelevant, instead of striving to revive a spiritual conviction and a conscience apart from the political mentality.

The British Council of Churches in April, 1958, received a report from one of its working committees recommending that churches "leave to others the extent to which it is expedient to amend the law on Sunday entertainment." The council said further that churches should concentrate on "the primary and urgent task" of educating their own members regarding the Christian observance of the Sabbath, and at the same time make known to the general public their views on the subject. This is different, then, from power politics and legislative lobbying. The action suggested by the BCC is not concerned with the mote in the brothers' eyes, but rather with educating its own brethren along the lines of acceptable principles. But here is a problem area for the church at large, too. What are acceptable principles?

4. *Reconsider the place of principles in Christian group action.*

Certain principles [4] tell us what to do. One tells us that man should rest on Sunday; another that he should enjoy himself if he is to glorify God; another principle would say to work on Sunday, if a person believes this is what he should do, if his job requires it, if his family support depends on it, or if it gives him (particularly if he is not a Christian) more enjoyment than attending Christian worship or following a Christian prescription for the day. One set of principles, highlighting the creation and the Ten Commandments, encourages Sabbath observers; another set of principles, highlighting the resurrection and other events of the New Testament, permits a transfer of the original idea of Sabbath. We are surrounded by principles. We have our moral principles. We believe in the principle of monogamy; yet others, including certain patriarchs of the Bible, believed in polygamy, while a shortage of women in Tibet today permits them to be polyandrous. Who is right? Is there such a thing as a universal principle, or do cultures change, becoming relevant to the time, their locus in history, and other conditions?

We may agree that principles of morality have been and possibly will be to a certain degree relevant; yet that which changes is not what we mean by principles. But how about inalienable rights and, in particular, the right to pursuit of happiness for all? Do such principles exist? How about religious liberty? Is there such a principle?

This seems like a rhetorical, unnecessary question. Of course, it can be argued that we need some principles like certain inalienable

---

[4] By principle, we mean an absolute, unchanging idea or ideal; an external criterion for evaluating the entire subjective and objective experience of man. If a principle changes, then it is not a principle. Principle in this book means that idea to which is ascribed metahistorical significance and permanence.

rights—freedom to worship, freedom from coercion, freedom to speak, and so on. Protestants speak emphatically of separation of church and state.

There is nothing objectionable about the principle of separation of church and state, but perhaps we could consider whether it is wrong for Christianity to be concerned with principles in the first place. The problem becomes understandable as we look at some recent statements of three groups, Roman Catholic, Protestant, and the Lord's Day Alliance.

Who said these?

[1] A church is a spiritual democracy to the degree that love and liberty rule. . . . Love is the royal law under which liberty is self-controlled for the largest good. . . . Religious liberty must be conceived in the light of the Christian world mission. . . . True freedom is Christian freedom. . . . Christian discipleship must express itself through love and obedience and witnessing. . . .

[2] A Christian politician has obligations to both the Church and the State and they should not be confused.

[3] We are . . . to create a good government founded upon the righteousness of God . . . for the Scripture tells us that "righteousness exalteth a nation."

There are many principles in the above, one after another—democracy, love, liberty, religious liberty, good discipleship, obedience. Then there is the principle of separation of church and state and also the recognition that there are separate principles of the church and the state that are binding on us. Lastly there are Biblical "principles" —love, freedom, righteousness of God. The above are all statements using absolutes to which Protestants would say "Amen." But could Catholics and political lobbyists adhere to these, too? The first statement is an excerpt from a Baptist study conference; the second by Roman Catholic Eugene McCarthy, senator from Minnesota; the third, by the Lord's Day Alliance.

Do you see now the problem of principles in this matter? We know that Protestants and Catholics and the Lord's Day Alliance have no real common ground for agreement. But they do agree—in principle. They can all adhere to the same principles. And adding an amen to the same principles above could be the Seventh-day Adventists, who believe they are being terribly persecuted by those not in agreement with them. But they do agree in principle. Take other principles—the brotherhood of man, equal rights, and so on. Fascists could agree with them, and one of the most blatant claims of Communism is that it recognizes the principle of brotherhood better than Christianity. "If you look into our philosophy," Soviet Premier Nikita Khrushchev told three thousand guests at a civic dinner in San Francisco in September, 1959, "you will see that we have taken a lot of Christian precepts, for example, 'Love Thy Neighbor.'" You see, we all agree in principle, but when these principles are interpreted there are hate, division, persecution, inquisition, torture.

Principles are like wolves in lamb's clothing. They are no place to begin solving problems. The same principles are shared by many— thus the church, if it wishes, can work just as well and with equal satisfaction and clarity of conscience with a Communist government as with a Western government. That is, when all parties appeal to principle. Says David Spitz: "For right action involves more than a recognition of right principles; it is more than merely intellectual. It derives most commonly from the emotions or, if you will, from the character of a man; it is a product of his opinions, of his attitudes, even more than of his learning or intelligence. This is why prejudice is so largely impervious to the appeal to the facts, why it is so little affected by reason." [5]

Principles are not communicable to the human situation. They are constantly distorted. An idea that is not communicable must remain entirely in another world, in a world of metaphysics or value, that never meets man on his level, as God does personally in Christ. And an idea that has no application or rapport is literally meaningless. The old ideas of the deists, of the eighteenth and nineteenth century enlightenment, are not subjects of the Christian faith.

The author pursued this line of thinking at the Baptist Conference on Religious Liberty sponsored by the Baptist Joint Committee on Public Affairs in Washington in September, 1958. The Baptists appealed to principles, such as love, as we saw above. But then two developments occurred at the conference that pointed a finger at these theologies governed by principles. I asked a small discussion group to which I was assigned, after listening to opinions as to what principles should apply in church-state relations, if any of the members had Sunday-closing battles in their communities. Immediately a Southern delegate replied, and the consensus of opinion supported him. He reported very effective action in his community to force Sunday closing.

"Does your church participate?" I asked.

"Yes, it does. We are doing everything we can to close down businesses on Sunday, and we're really making headway."

"Do you have Jews, Seventh-day Adventists in your community?"

"Yes, but they are not strong enough to give us any trouble."

"Do you think we as Baptists ought to act that way?"

Only one out of the group was forthright in answering No. Several did not know—the rest defended Sunday restriction laws. Then, before going on to a further discussion, I suggested we take any passage in the study document on the Biblical basis for religious freedom, and point out where at all it differed from any statement coming from the Vatican, or for that matter from Colombia where there had been frequent reports of the persecuting and slaying of Protestants. The conclusion was wholly obvious. We were saying the very same thing as the Roman Catholics and behaving just as they are accused of doing, appealing to power politics, and persecuting a minority to the degree of refusing equal rights for the minority, and overtly persecuting them by fines and imprisonment if they dared to challenge the Protestant-Catholic sanctioned laws.

It was several days before I got back to the Conference on Religious Liberty sessions. It was now the last morning session. Questions were received from the floor, and two men in particular introduced some fireworks to the session. They were Reuben E. Alley, editor of the *Religious Herald* (Southern Baptist State paper for Virginia), and H. Wadell Waters, pastor of the First Baptist Church, Virginia Beach, Virginia. Dr. Alley referred to the action of the Southern Baptist executive committee in reference to the Hill-Burton Act providing funds for hospital construction. "Someone appeared as a Southern Baptist before a Congressional committee," he said, "to protest the Hill-Burton Act, and when our pleas were rejected, the Southern Baptist then turned around and said, 'If you are going to give out this money, we need to be included, too.' The principles were made worthless in practice."

In his remarks before the conference, Waters, who also is chairman of the Religious Liberty Study Committee, Baptist General Association of Virginia, poured some real salt on the problem: "The consensus of this meeting seems to be: It's OK to collaborate with the government where money is involved, while there are Baptists in this group who find it heretical and satanic to cooperate with one another." It was all right to trust the state, but not one another.

As the members of the Virginia delegations were beginning to pierce the unity of the meeting, it began to be clear that we were really back where we started. For the various speakers appealed to the eternal principle of church-state separation and that of total religious liberty and rights of man that needed no adaptation. I countered with a question: "How is desegration coming?" I asked. This was back in the fall of 1958. I got a general answer. Then I switched to Sunday laws. The delegate was all in favor of abolishing them, recognizing the rights of the minority along the lines of what had been said by his group.

"Is your church desegrated?"

"Oh, no."

"How about the rights of the Negro?" I asked.

It was explained that this was different.

So while his Baptist brethren from the official Baptist headquarters in Nashville were guilty of terrible duplicity, there was a "beam" in his own eye. In fact, there is always a beam in our own eyes—that is, when we appeal to principles. Let us refrain from talking of abstract principles—for they permit compromise with prejudices and vested interests and merely give us sanctions for persecution.

Principles are one thing that we cannot avoid bringing into our everyday conversation and reasoning. They are a part of our make-up. But we must take principles with a grain of salt; and if one thing is certain for Christians, if there is an absolute, it is the dictum that there is no absolute. Says Kenneth W. Thompson, Assistant Director for the Social Sciences at the Rockefeller Foundation: "If there is an absolute in the realm of political ethics, it is that no single proximate moral standard, whether self-determination or the

United Nations, can be held up as an absolute." [6] Nor does Christian evangelical religion have a place for the absolutes, but rather for experience, a knowledge of a person, a Savior. This idea can be made into a principle, an object, but it is then a perversion of the faith. Christians depend on the presence of a personality, that of Jesus, not on principles. "Timeless principles belong more to Greek thought than to Hebraic thought, more to Idealism than to Christianity," [7] says the Reverend G. B. Mather, Saskatoon, Saskatchewan, in the 1957 annual report of the Board of Evangelism and Social Service of The United Church of Canada. If the church could learn to express itself in terms of personality and in concern for all personality— all individuals—it would have a solution, at least a constructive course in regard to Sunday laws, as compared to the negative assertion of principles.

Now in regard to the problem of principles and the role that principles play in compromise (there can be no compromise or synthesis, really, without assertion of principles), the church might take four courses of action:

(a) *Do not assert principles* (even if the church insists on recognizing principles). The church will have unchanging ideals; it will have standards. But the church must not look to them. It needs to look beyond them. For a Christian group, action should emerge from a response to Christ, not to principles or ideals. "For Jesus, good living is the spontaneous activity of a transformed character; for the Scribes and Pharisees it is obedience to a discipline, imposed from without." [8] Let the church, if it must enforce anything, enforce qualities of the spiritual life, indefinable, creative, variable qualities. Enforcing universal precepts such as the idea of a Sabbath or the more precise defined standard, a Sunday Lord's Day, can be disastrous to the creation of a constructive, spiritually effective society. "To enforce any religion's particular standards upon the general community,"

[6] Kenneth W. Thompson, "Prophets and Politics," in *What the Christian Hopes for in Society* (New York: Association Press, 1957), p. 111.

[7] G. B. Mather, "Biblical Teaching Regarding Beverage Alcohol," in *God's Will for Our Time*, 32nd Annual Report of the Board of Evangelism and Social Service of The United Church of Canada, 1957, p. 132.

[8] Thomas W. Manson, *The Teaching of Jesus* (New York: The Macmillan Company, 1932), p. 300.

says William Clancy, education director, Church Peace Union, "either through law or pressure, can only increase the division with which our society is already torn." [9] Said Benjamin Franklin: "When a religion is good, I conceive that it will support itself; and, when it cannot support itself, and God does not take care to support it, so that its professors are obliged to call for the help of the civil power, it is a sign, I apprehend, of its being a bad one.[10]

Let the church speak precisely, concretely, but let it do so without principles. When principles enter the discussion, let the conclusion come without the aid of a "time-honored" or permanent ideal which we call principle. "Imprecise necessities—like the words 'conservative,' 'freedom,' 'religion'—ought to be used imprecisely," says Peter Viereck, professor of Modern European History at Holyoke College. "Reality itself is unsymmetrical, ungeometrical, imprecise." Conservatism's "most valuable insights are not sustained theoretical works nor well-organized, clearly presented, and geometrically consistent treatises, as in the case of liberal rationalism. Rather its most valuable insights are the quick thrusts of epigrams, as in the writings of Metternich, Disraeli, Tocqueville, Burkhardt, Churchill, or the nuggets concealed within the disorganized, wonderfully helter-skelter jottings of Coleridge, the most imaginative, most incoherent conservative of them all." [11] Let the church then speak with jabs, quips, and not with invariable principles.

(b) *Begin with the human predicament.* It may be said that to do so, we begin with certain ecclesiastical principles; namely, sin, guilt, loneliness. But what determines these religious precepts? Are they really principles? Does a cow sin? Is a monkey guilty? Is a grasshopper lonely? Put these questions on a human level. Is a gangster, the head of the mafia, really sinful, guilty, lonely? What brings in these ideas? It is God, and namely a participating, suffering God that can convict men of their sins, create an idea of guilt, confront them with themselves, the uncertainties of existence, creating loneliness. Christian standards or directions or goals are purely relative.

[9] William Clancy, "Religion as a Source of Tension," *Religion and the Free Society,* p. 33.

[10] John Bigelow, editor, *The Works of Benjamin Franklin,* Vol. 8, DCCCXXIV, "To Richard Price" (New York: G. P. Putnam's Sons, 1904), p. 311.

[11] Peter Viereck, "The Inarticulate Roots of Free Values," in the *Christian Scholar,* June, 1958, pp. 159, 160.

They do not begin with Greek cosmology, essences, ideals, potentialities. Our action, our thinking, decisions, cohesions within society come from our experience, emotion, the inner self. Let the church begin anew—begin with Christ, and work toward its solutions. Its confrontation with society might vary from age to age—from an agrarian society all the way to a Space-Age pluralistic society, and even then, there would be variation from the 1960's to the 1980's.

(c) *Respect multiple principles rather than single principles* (if the church organization in its daily life insists on operating by some principle). As I write this I have just received a bulletin of the "legislative information service of the Illinois Council of Churches." Consider two excerpts—the first dealing with a House bill prohibiting distribution of obscene literature to persons under the age of eighteen, and the second with a House bill prohibiting business on Sunday except the sale of food, drugs, gasoline, and certain other articles.

Now consider the proposed action of the church, or rather the advice of the church group in each instance. Concerning the obscene-literature bill:

The Committee agreed that this was a good bill in principle, believing in the prohibition of obscene literature. However, there is a need for more rigid legislation which would make it illegal to publish and distribute, as well as sell such literature *at any age* level. To protect the youth of our state it would be wise to support this bill and work for greater control of this situation within the local community.

Concerning the Sunday restrictive legislation:

The Committee indicates its support with the intent of the bill and with any attempt to suspend the conduct of business on Sunday. However, the bill would be improved if it were more rigid in regard to exemption of certain businesses. (Grocery stores and liquor stores are not included in this legislation.) . . . It will be helpful to indicate to legislators that the principle of such legislation is good, but that it would be more effective to include all businesses except those which are considered emergency items.

Note the appeal to principles in both cases. Note also that in both cases the appeal is to a single, unique principle. In both cases equally important principles are overlooked. In regard to the obscene-literature bill, we could raise questions concerning freedom from government monopoly and censorship of the mail. A very significant, important principle. In regard to the Sunday-legislation proposal, what shall we say about the principle of the separation of church and state, the principle of nonestablishment of religion, the principle of religious freedom? Are these any less important than a unilateral application of a religious principle that calls for Sabbath observance? When a church speaks in terms of a single principle, or a single subject, it is not speaking as a Christian church. If it must speak (because of its involvement in society and sinful nature) in terms of principles instead of the terms of experiential theology and the questions of existence, let it speak in reference to multiple principles.

How would a specific church group speak in regard to the above matters? Concerning obscene literature, let it present all principles and suggest actions that do not depend on any one principle or rather that do not violate the principles of others. Let the church suggest directions for individual actions—how one might persuade by various means the local distributor, or vote, or influence those who vote. The position of a church group is to enlighten the individual. Perhaps he would prefer censorship over a deluge of immoral literature in his community; perhaps he would prefer the filthy literature over censorship. The question is not one for the church to decide. The same is true with Sunday laws. The issue may be a little clearer with Sunday regulation, for the church need not decide between immorality and censorship. The church can be on the side of morality, anticensorship, brotherhood, and many other desirable principles, if it diametrically opposes Sunday legislation. But if, for traditional reasons and strong convictions, it feels that it must maintain the past way of doing things, then let the church again present a host of alternatives to its constituents, rather than one principle. The church could go further, after considering all principles, such as the rights of the individual, the businessman, the religious exceptions, the welfare of the community, certain philosophical principles such as that which says there is no real change and that which says all is flux, that which is subjective, that which is wholly objective, and so on. After such consideration, the church then would be closer to the kingdom of Jesus than it would be with unilateral enforcement of single principles. Concretely, if this regard for a multiplicity of principles be the action of the church, various church groups might suggest a two-day Sabbath to civil authorities to allow for the rights of the minorities. Our rest period is already longer than Sunday in the United States. The church could be up to date and solve some of the Saturday-Sunday worship dilemmas by campaigning for a weekend closing.[12] India, Russia, Yugoslavia, for instance, have one-and-one-half-day closings (Saturday afternoon and Sunday). Or the church might suggest that a business elect any one day (or days) in the week to close, or alternate as to which ones are to be open on Sunday, as ministers eventually recommended in Fort Dodge, Iowa, as a compromise solution to across-the-board Sunday openings. Discussion among competitors might result in closing on Sunday, as the car dealers of San Diego, Nashville, and Tucson agreed to do. Or if sales were better on Sunday, they might agree to close on some other day.

With New York City's large minorities, if a weekend closing was not achieved, it would be feasible to consider letting a person choose his own day. This might appear to be chaos, but it would not be near the chaos of the current situation. It is hard to enforce the current law among the massive Jewish population of the East Side of New York. "The number of areas involved would be very small," according to a member of the American Jewish Committee. "It would be easier to license the exceptions than to have the whole city in chaos over a law that cannot be applied uniformly or effectively."[13]

Recognizing a multiplicity of principles permits the church to

[12] In New Zealand, when the forty-hour week was introduced in the mid-thirties, the result was the closing of almost all shops for the whole of Saturday and Sunday. People simply had to get used to purchasing their groceries, etc., for a "long weekend." Stores selling milk were permitted to remain open on Saturday and Sunday, but usually they restricted their own opening times. And all of this happened in a nation where only a minority of homes had refrigerators. Admittedly, almost all people had milk delivered to the door daily. And refrigerators are now much more common—almost universal—in New Zealand, even as they are in the United States.

[13] This special licensing of establishments works in England, as regulated by the Shops Act of 1950. Generally the Act provides that every shop shall, save as otherwise provided by the Act, be closed for the serving of customers on Sunday (Section 47). Section 53 of the Act provides that the occupier of any shop who is a person of the Jewish religion shall be entitled, upon making to the local authority an application in accordance with the provisions of this Section, to have the shop registered by the local authority and so long as it is so registered then (a) the shop shall be closed for all purposes connected with trade or business on Saturday and (b) the shop may remain open until 2 o'clock on Sunday and (c) a notice conspicuously placed in the shop will state that it will be closed on Saturday and open on Sunday until 2:00 P.M.

leave in the hands of the secular powers—management, unions, the state—the decisions and formulation of all labor legislation. The church, ridding itself of its own vested interests, can suggest legislation that is in keeping with the widest range of principles, considering the Jew as it considers itself.

(d) *Speak in terms of "limits."* No longer should the church talk of certain values of the Christian life, that is, values as objects determined by principles. Consider rest values. As we have already asked: Is any single idea of rest valid for all individuals? The church says that a rest day is necessary. Science simply states that different individuals need different amounts of sleep and inactivity.

One can work every day of the year and live to be a hundred, or he can observe the Sabbath and die in his teens, and vice versa. Each person has his own limits. Now the church can talk in terms of limits. G. G. Berkouwer, professor at the Free University of Amsterdam, insists that our actions must be conditioned by limits set by revelation.[14] In agreeing with him we have to be sure that revelation does not mean a revelation of principles or laws. Barth, for instance, believes that revelation, or rather the author of revelation, God through His word, is the starting point. But this is such an objective concept for him that revelation becomes a code of laws, grace becomes the ground of demands. Wingren, commenting on the weakness of Barth at this point, says: "Law cannot be vanquished by the gospel. The danger inherent in Barth's conception is that the gospel which bestows, not demands, righteousness loses its essential content. In its place there is a revelation of God in Christ, a revelation which supplied man's lack of knowledge of God; and from this kind of revelation it is possible to derive rules and regulations for human life." [15]

The Gospel does not become a principle giving birth to new laws; it is not a postscript to legalism, with its own legalism; it stands in tension with all principles, all ideas of justice. A person living under grace through the power of the Holy Spirit forms his own limits.

A person can live wholly without principles, as Caligula, in Albert Camus' play by the same name, tried to do. Caligula is free to do

[14] L. B. Smedes, "Significant Theological Works," *Christianity Today*, Feb. 16, 1959, p. 4.

[15] Wingren, *op. cit.*, p. 128.

what he pleases. Yet there were limits to what he could do. (There were limits in the life of Camus, too, as his tragic death in a speeding Facel Vega sports car in 1960 indicates.) There was just so much murder and destruction Caligula could bring before his fate caught up with him. "Give a person enough rope and he will hang himself," says an idiom. Caligula rebelled. A reckless, greedy young man, he was so conceited, he would claim everything for himself. Like Jezebel and Ahab of the Old Testament, he forgot that he would have to face himself. Happiness was not for the asking. Camus thus has a tragic, pathetic end for Caligula, capitulating beneath the thrust of daggers after four short years as emperor of Rome. Camus describes Caligula's scene of realization, as he turns suddenly to face a mirror as he leaves the gasping, dying form of Caesonia, his mistress, whom he has slowly strangled:

Caligula! You, too; you, too, are guilty. Then what of it—a little more, a little less? Yet who can condemn me in this world where there is no judge, where nobody is innocent? . . . I've stretched out my hands (his voice rises to a scream); see, I stretch out my hands, but it's always you I find, you only, confronting me, and I've come to hate you. I have chosen a wrong path, a path that leads to nothing. My freedom isn't the right one . . . (He . . . hurls the stool at it [the mirror], screaming). To history, Caligula! Go down to history! (The mirror breaks and at the same moment armed conspirators rush in. Caligula swings round to face them with a mad laugh. Scipio and Cherea, who are in front, fling themselves at him and stab his face with their daggers. Caligula's laughter turns to gasps. All strike him, hurriedly, confusedly. In a last gasp, laughing and choking, Caligula shrieks) I'm still alive! [16]

The religionist would say you cannot violate God's laws forever; the court of justice would say that crime does not pay—that principles of justice cannot be avoided; Camus simply says there are limits to how far anyone can go. He refutes Kant's moral imperatives, but ends with almost the same thing, without principles. Thus in recognizing the development of limits out of activity, Camus is very close to the traditional views.

Living without principles, without values, appears frightening. "One who knows or who observes no restraints on his impulses and

[16] Albert Camus, *Caligula and Three Other Plays*, translated by Stuart Gilbert (New York: Alfred A. Knopf, 1958), pp. 72–74.

desires is of necessity an arbitrary ruler, for he tends always to go to the limit of his power." [17] Living without values and principles begets immorality, crime. That is, except where there is Christ. For one can live with a relativist philosophy, coming to recognize a panorama of limits rather than fixed eternal principles, if he has a corrective. And for the Christian, the corrective in his new, total freedom is the corrective of Christ. Limits mean there is an end to something. The Christian church can see the darkness—its light must be rekindled, it must move on. The church sees the limit of something—it moves on, conquering the darkness, and as long as there are enough aggressive Christian spirits, the earth emits bright spots all over. But even then, darkness always closes in and continually changes the situation. Yet the church can push on, establishing new limits.

For example, we have certain principles of evangelism, but they change or should change—India will not open its doors to a missionary unless he also qualifies in a secular field; Africa is becoming the same way. China is completely closed, except perhaps for indirect influence; in the old days in the United States the tent and the revival were sure formulas for successful evangelism; now there are new media. A church pushes toward new limits. Capital punishment looks different to the church in the last half of the twentieth century in the United States than it did to Jewish-Christian churches in the first century. When a church is without principles, precise value judgments, it can enter into the most urgent situation. Its decision will come out of its participation in that situation. In regard to the Sunday laws there would be no principles or values that would have any meaning for the church except that which it can derive from the immediate situation in which it lives and in which it communes with its Savior. If such be the case, then pronouncements on the blue laws will never come down from general councils or conventions. The church can recognize the limits and application of its faith in a society. The decisions are with church communicants, each one in interaction with his Savior, not an anonymous group in interaction with permanent principles. William Phillips, commenting on Ignazio Silone's recent novel *The Secret of Luca,* says: "Human safeguards are

[17] David Spitz, *op. cit.,* p. 5.

to be found in the authenticity of individual men rather than in the movements dedicated to mankind." [18]

WHAT CAN INDIVIDUAL CHRISTIANS DO?

First of all, we cannot suggest general courses for all Christians—this is not the matter of a book writer, a preacher, a church body, a world congress. Nevertheless, when we are considering a problem on which responsible Christian action is desired, then it is possible to give some precise Christian answers, without a degree of finality. The finality and the judgment must rest with God. But individual Christians, speaking as individuals, will have something to say to specific issues. The prophets spoke as individuals; they spoke with conviction; they spoke to the issues.

Could the individual take a cue from the foregoing advice for church bodies? For the individual makes up the church group. Therefore he can cast his vote or use his personal influence or persuasion to support the action of a group that minimizes compromise. He can encourage novelty in church policy and watch to see that a compromised action does not become a permanent thing. He can avoid asserting principles, preferring to keep his religion and statements of faith in an experiential area. But if certain principles emerge, such as what is right and proper on Sunday, he should seek to introduce other principles such as brotherhood, love, freedom, the separation of church and state.

Should the individual be for or against Sunday laws? He should be neither for nor against anything in general. After considering all principles and data involved, he could evolve a reasonable opinion. Better still, if he could consider himself in a standpoint with no special interest, if he could close his eyes on all the principles he has been taught, and open his eyes in faith, constructing and selecting his own goals, he might evolve an answer that is wholly radical, one that may go against the grain of the currently popular principles but one that is spiritually exciting and convincing to him.

[18] William Phillips, "Men and History: The Tragic Visions of Pasternak and Silone," *Commentary Magazine*, December, 1958, p. 532.

If a Christian acts out of response to Christ, forsaking dependence on singular arbitrary principles:

He might oppose blue laws radically. He could not find many new reasons or arguments beyond those normally offered. His main reason for opposing Sunday laws would be that he finds them spiritually repulsive—or, to be more reserved, he would say that he is not satisfied with favoring certain principles at the exclusion of other principles, and to push the matter further, he would wonder if any principles with permanence are valid for the Christian.

He might de-emphasize the Ten Commandments. There are other things for Christians to talk about, namely, the new life in Christ. What Luther said about the fourth commandment (Lutheran third) we would apply to all—the Sabbath "is abrogated in the New Testament. . . . Paul expressly abrogates the sabbath." [19] There is not any of the commandments that we really keep—we change the Sabbath, we kill when we feel like it, by capital punishment, by wars. Our very thoughts, according to Jesus, break the rest of them. Protestants and Catholics cannot agree on what the Ten Commandments are. (Roman Catholics and Lutherans split the last one, but combine the first two as one.) Roger Williams placed them in two categories—four are spiritual, the rest are secular. But that is beside the point. The Protestant has no real use for them. He is content to let the matter of Sunday action rest on a much more inclusive and relevant note, where Jesus put it: "Thou shalt love the Lord thy God with all thy heart, and with all thy soul, and with all thy mind. This is the first and great commandment. And the second is like unto it, Thou shalt love thy neighbour as thyself. On these two commandments hang all the law and the prophets." [20] Love God and love your neighbor, even your enemy, the nonmember of your own circle, as Jesus expanded the idea in his discourse.[21]

He might accept a suffering role in society. This is hard for an individual to do, but it would be a test of his faith. A governor pointed out to me, rather crudely, that the righteous have the privilege of suffering, when, in defending blue laws, he exclaimed that

---

[19] Conrad Bergendoff and Helmut T. Lehman, editors, *Luther's Works,* Vol. 40, *Church and Ministry,* "Against the Heavenly Prophets" (Philadelphia: Muhlenberg Press, 1958), p. 93.

[20] Matthew 22:37–40.

[21] Matthew 5:44.

"the Jews have a right to suffer." He proceeded to explain that the proponent of true religion always has the right to suffer. He referred to the Mormons—they are obligated to give 10 percent, thus suffering financially. Though shocked at first by an apparent lack of sensitivity for the minorities, I realized later that what the governor was saying was true. The religious, whether they have a right to do so or not, often do suffer. The Orthodox Jew, the sincere Adventist, the Muslim in a Christian country, the Christian in Cairo does pay a price for his faith. It is so often the case. "For so persecuted they the prophets which were before you." [22] The bearing of the cross, no matter how small or how great it might be in a community, standing up against the popular religious mentality, is a mark of a religious man. The Jew therefore opposes blue laws with a sincere conviction and joy. The joy can also belong to the Christian. He can stand up courageously against the prevailing religious mentality of his peers, preferring multiple principles, and better still no principles, in a life sincerely committed to the Person of Christ. Is it then a simpler matter than we anticipated, that commitment to Christ and dependence on *sola gratia* ("grace only") are the church's alternatives to the specter of an Inquisition in a Space Age?

[22] Matthew 5:12.

VI SEARCH FOR A DAY

Christians do not have to worship on Sunday. "Now that our Lord has come and begun a new, eternal kingdom throughout the world, we Christians are no longer bound to such external, specific observance. On the contrary, we have the liberty to turn Monday or some other day of the week into Sunday if the Sabbath or Sunday does not please us." [1] Yet Christians have adhered to the Jewish idea that one day should be holy to the Lord. In the Space Age, if that formality is retained, what day should it be?

What the church decides will have a terrific impact on the Sunday controversies across the United States and Canada, for if church thinking continues to support the need for Sunday closing, then the battles will be fought more furiously in the near future, as the age and mood of the times change, with perhaps the prestige of the church and its spiritual influence being the price; if, however, the church in its theological reconsiderations finds Sunday is adaptable or dispensable in favor of another alternative, then there would be no religious or moral sanction for retaining Sunday legislation. As the state heeds its majority voice, which in a democracy it must, then that majority voice, if it seeks to assert itself politically as it has in the past, may beat the path to another day or arrangement of days. If the church majority, representing a wide Christian cohesion, shows signs of defection and changing, then obviously the state also would, in

[1] Martin Luther in a sermon at the dedication of the Castle Church at Torgau, Oct. 5, 1544, quoted in *What Luther Says*, compiled by Ewald M. Plass (St. Louis: Concordia Publishing House, 1959), p. 1329.

regard to the amount of restrictive legislation it passes concerning a particular religious holy day.

In considering premises for a holy day in the Space Age, a point that cannot escape us, when we look at the Scriptures, is that the Bible deals with two covenants and that each covenant is made with a certain group of persons, not with an abstract group or a past generation. The covenant is personal. The writer of Deuteronomy says: "The Lord made not this covenant with our fathers, but with us, even us, who are all of us here alive this day." [2] The covenant is continually renewed, or reintroduced on different terms as with the New Testament, and it involves each individual. To the Christian, entrance into the promises of the New Covenant is through a new birth, his own individual experience with the Covenanter. In the New Covenant he will not have the same concerns of the Jew who remembered the Sabbath because it was commanded on Sinai as a memorial of creation and/or a memorial of the exodus from Egypt. The New Covenant introduces new elements to commemorate.

Now, what do we want to remember in the Space Age about our Covenant and the central facts of it? This is the place to begin in searching for a day. What do we want to highlight about our faith in the Space Age? What pattern of commemoration will strengthen us as Christians and best communicate the Gospel of Jesus Christ?

In reference to days, as we saw in the third chapter, we have a starting point in the Bible and in the writers of the early church. Although daily emphasis was the practice at first, certain days received emphasis by the early Christians. By the time of Constantine, these days were primarily three—Friday, in memory of the crucifixion; Saturday, the day of rest and preparation remembering the creation and the exodus; and Sunday, the day of the resurrection.

We could also select as starting points the birth of Jesus, his incarnation as a whole, his healing or teaching ministry, his resurrection, his ascension. Any of these. You have your preference. History has its preference.

For the Space Age this author would like to suggest, if a single day is to be selected, a day of the cross, for these reasons:

1. *Redemption is centered in the cross.*

[2] Deuteronomy 5:3.

Our century has gone in many directions theologically—at its beginning, the idealism of the past century was still prevalent. Realism entered after the First World War. Then came the American version of orthodoxy which had influenced Europe through Karl Barth's *Commentary on Romans* and *Church Dogmatics,* with the realization that society is imperfect and that the only hope for man was through the proclamation of the Gospel of Jesus Christ. And what is the Gospel of Jesus Christ?

It is the good news that Jesus is the Redeemer of men, the promised Messiah, the Son that "sitteth on the right hand of God" as a perpetual intercessor for men. What is this good news without the cross? What is it for Barth, if the cross is taken out of the authoritative word of God, if the cross is taken from the unilateral action of God toward man—there would be no New Testament, only the words and chronicle of another prophet. What would the good news be without the cross for Brunner and Niebuhr as they contemplate the sinfulness of men? for Nygren, who finds the answers to his philosophical questions in the essence of Calvary? for Bultmann, whose proclamation of the kerygma or Gospel message meets man understandably in his own momentary helplessness before a yawning abyss? for popular preacher-theologians, such as Ferré, and preachers from Preston Bradley to Ralph Sockman for whom love or agape becomes an idea derived from or heightened by Calvary? What, for that matter, would the other elements of Christendom besides Protestantism, the theology of Anglicanism, Roman Catholicism, Eastern Orthodoxy, be without the cross?

The Roman Catholic Mass emphasizes the significant sacrifice on the cross; the proclamation of the Protestant pulpit brings this anew to the Protestant congregation in revival meetings and in more formal settings. Christian faith, and the assurance of the rewards of that faith—salvation, redemption—begin with the sacrifice of God's Son for sinners on the cross.

Before there can be a conclusion to a story there must be a climax. Before there can be resurrection there must be death— death of sin, death eventually of the body. The "promise of life is also a demand for readiness to accept death."[3] Life for the Chris-

[3] Rudolf Bultmann, "Theology for Freedom and Responsibility," *Christian Century,* Aug. 27, 1958, p. 967.

tian begins with death; it begins with the cross, and leads into resurrection.

A day to be observed as a regular Christian holy day should recognize this central fact of the cross, remembering in the gathering the one occasion that Jesus enjoined us to remember, "This is my body, which is broken for you." [4]

2. *The cross brings meaning to the contemporary age.*

The cross answers the question which Berdyaev (as well as Unamuno, Forsyth, Camus, and others) poses over and over again: "How is the existence of an almighty and all-gracious God to be reconciled with the evil and suffering that are in the world?" [5] When we begin with the Jewish Sabbath, recognizing it as a day of creation, then we have an interplanetary metaphysics, vague, but up to date, as we ascribe everything in the world to God. But unfortunately, as up to date as the affirmation of God as creator is in our day of marvelous new discoveries in the universe, the affirmation is not a Christian one. For Christianity is interested in a God who exists, who lives, who suffers with man, rather than a God who is a doting architect, creating and setting the hands of the clock. The terrible holocaust of recent years, and the possibility of new terrors, the fact that poverty still exists externally and internally in the hearts of men, indicate that a God who speaks to suffering mankind must be a God who is cognizant of suffering. The most realistic picture of the world is not one of optimism and idealism alone but a recognition of the tragic roles we all play. We are all sinners and we all shall die, and there are demonic forces challenging a participating God. "Christianity views the cosmos realistically, then, as pervaded by tragic elements and in need of redemption all together. Christianity not only leads us to be realistic in our thinking, however, but also helps us to have the courage to see the constructive side of these otherwise tragic elements, in the universe." [6] Thus when Christianity realizes that it originated in the depths of despair, of Christ anguishing in the garden, that it is a religion of a bleeding

[4] 1 Corinthians 11:24.

[5] Nicholas Berdyaev, *Truth and Revelation* (New York: Harper and Brothers, 1953), p. 98.

[6] Jack Finegan, *Space, Atoms, and God* (St. Louis: The Bethany Press, 1959), p. 44.

Redeemer—when this is realized, then Christians can hardly underestimate the place of the cross in their faith. Suffering is the way of
life for the Christian. "All that will live godly in Christ Jesus shall
suffer persecution." [7]

3. *The cross is the best point of reference for communication
with modern Space-Age man.*

Is the cross a better point of communication than the resurrection, with which Sunday has traditionally been linked? The resurrection has always been inconceivable to the man estranged from God.
So has the fact that God's very Son was crucified on earth. Both
of these emphases are a *skandalon*, "stumbling block," to the irreligious man, such as a Communist. How does one approach a Communist? Does the Christian have a philosophy of history that is as
thoroughgoing as Hegel's? Would the spirit of history, as the Christian sees it, be an answer to the Communist's spirit of history? Perhaps this would be possible, for evangelism begins sometimes with
similarities. But how similar are the two spirits of history? One is
really a dialectic of the material, an anonymous spirit or force at
best. The other, the Christian, is the definite Spiritual involvement
of God. Actually, then, anonymity is facing the Spirit of God. We
are a gulf apart, and the Communist cannot heed us, and he certainly
does not flock into our churches.

We do not really try to communicate with the Communist. And
there is no real encouragement. According to an April 14, 1959, report in the New York *Times*, Pope John XXIII "forbade Roman
Catholics throughout the world . . . to vote for candidates or parties that supported or gave comfort to the communists." The article,
by Arnaldo Cortesi also reports that Pope John's predecessor, Pius
XII, had "excommunicated all militant Communists on June 1, 1949."
Communism and Christianity, Roman or otherwise, are not recon-
cilable, at least as far as the Western church is concerned. Barth
would maintain that Christianity is even less compatible with capi-
talistic materialism, but that is beside the point. The fact that Christianity and Communism are incompatible does not mean that we
should lose any attempts to evangelize the Communist. With this
we agree. But what shall be the emphasis? Remember that we are

[7] 2 Timothy 3:12.

dealing, not with unadulterated atheism, but die-hard devotees to materialism and a materialistic process. Should we talk to them about the resurrection? the afterlife, the risen Savior? or would we make more headway with the Communists, and the other unevangelized masses of the world, by beginning with the crucifixion?

Russian Communists, it is said, are very much impressed by Jesus of Nazareth who was crucified on Calvary. But they are quite unimpressed with the Christ of "Christian theology." They start by rejecting any thought of "miracle"—and what greater miracle is there than the resurrection?

With the crucifixion, we are not starting with a claim contrary to the materialistic standpoint. With such a starting point, we nevertheless still present the nonbeliever with a *skandalon*. To expect a person to believe that the Son of God actually was put to death on the earth is no mean expectation. Any starting point would demand some "leap of faith." But for the individual who experiences anxiety, for the millions in slavery to a commune or party system, there is something in Christian theology that speaks to his situation, that Christ also was made like men, and died on a cross. And this reference to the cross can lead into hope and into the idea of resurrection by faith. The cross does not ignore the human predicament— it meets man where he is, assures him that Christ too has suffered, that he has also entered life, and that because of this death experience and the hand of God there is new life.

Actually, when we speak of the cross and death of the Son of God we are not really speaking of a paradox. Paul Tillich makes this point in the second volume of his *Systematic Theology*. A paradox is that which runs contrary to a fact. For example, would the fact that God's Son died on a cross be a paradox? It runs against the common opinion that a Son of God should not die. Tillich says No, that such a wish is not critically founded. The fact that God is supposed to triumph is an opinion, one which a Communist may refer to but himself has no faith in. Reference to the suffering of the God-man is no real paradox, for it contradicts nothing but mere opinion. So the Christian talking in terms of the historical death of Christ, of God's Son, is not really talking in terms of a paradox.

The cross permits the Christian to speak in terms that are understandable, and historically acceptable. It permits him to speak specifically. Christ is not a vague presence—he was incarnate, and more than that, subject to trials and tribulations as we are. He was cruci-fied. Christianity by beginning with the cross has a key to signifi-cance in the Space Age. "As man beholds the perfect, suffering love of God shining through the face of Jesus Christ he begins to see the magnitude of his own sin and cries out for forgiveness." [8]

The point of communication ought to be taken seriously by the church whose main existence visibly is justified by the fact that it is an organ of communication of the Gospel. To evangelize, the problems of communication must be kept in mind, and in selecting a day of worship, consideration ought to be given not only to the chief emphases of the church but also to what it wants to com-municate to the community— Do we want to say that Christ is alive, or that Christ is a Savior, or rather that Christ is a Savior and that he lives?

The cross is the logical starting point, for death must precede resurrection. The cross is relevant to the situation, the hopelessness, the guilt, the anxiety of the individual. It speaks to the suffering on the level of suffering. Being historically or at least literally verifi-able, it is not really a valid paradox in the human situation. Also, the cross provides significant reference in the language of men. On the mission field or in the small rural revival, recalling the event of Calvary permits fertile ground for the working of the Holy Spirit.

We have questioned whether there be a resurrection without a cross, whether the dénouement is more important than the climax. We will not go so far as to say that the cross is more important than the resurrection, but we do recognize the importance of the cross in God's plan of redemption, his communion with man, the fact that the cross is an important factor in communicating the Gospel among men and that it is a premise for establishing and affirming in faith the resurrection.

The tendency today in theology is not to separate any of these factors or to highlight them, but to speak in terms of the incarnation. Barth, for instance, sets a pace by emphasizing the incarnation rather than the resurrection or the cross. Aulén emphasizes the cross by

[8] Walter N. Stockburger, "The Relevance of the Gospel," in the *Religious Herald,* Dec. 4, 1958, p. 4.

first emphasizing the whole incarnation as sacrifice.[9] The difficulty of this over-all approach is that when one is concerned with the whole life of Jesus, then each word, each deed, each action has significance. And in emphasizing everything, we find ourselves clinging to every iota of the life of Jesus. Theology becomes a code of laws or, for the nonevangelical, a code of generalized and embodied principles. And the Christian is under a new code more foreboding than the old.

The difficulties are even greater in the Space Age. What about the problem of communication? How do you communicate the incarnation? The mythology is great—God becomes flesh. This is the Greek formula. With it one can easily lose track of a participating, involved Redeemer. In fact, one wonders, if the incarnation is so important per se, why Jesus did not live to be sixty or seventy years old. The reason is that his task was not to give birth to a new code of ethics but rather to accomplish certain feats—a death and a resurrection. These cannot be eclipsed by the incarnation. The whole quality of the new birth, of Christian experience, and the question of communication elicit an emphasis on the climax of the faith, the cross at Calvary, and its God-decreed correlative, the resurrection.

An emphasis on the "fragments" of the life of Christ has been called divisive, more recently by George S. Hendry in his *The Gospel of the Incarnation*. He says that serious differences have risen because of emphases on fragments of the Gospel; namely, the death and resurrection. An emphasis on Easter, he says, leads to pietism and mysticism; an emphasis on Calvary leads to orthodoxy. These emphases split the East and West, the Roman and the Eastern church. Fragmentary emphases have split the church continually. But what of it? Is there really evil in fragmentation? Or is it possible that the church is more alive when there are divisions, when there are two feet instead of one, many fingers, and so on? The body of Christ is broken, but not by fragmentary emphases as an ecumenical rhetoric maintains. The broken body of Christ is the result of the sins of men, of which we might suggest that unification of the church (and there was a central dominating church in Jesus' day) was one of the sins. If we must speak of incarnation, let us

[9] Gustaf Aulén, *Eucharist and Sacrifice* (Philadelphia: Muhlenberg Press, 1958), p. 148.

speak of it in the present tense, catching something of the repetition not only of Christ's words but also of his acts, a sense of his real or extenuated presence, as the Lutherans conceive of it in the sacrament of the Lord's Supper, or a perpetual immolation, as the mass conceives of it, or as the Protestant revivalist has caught it, presenting not an idolized Christ, but a participating Incarnate Christ, whose death on the cross can cleanse persons from sins. Arthur H. Kolsti caught the significance of the incarnation for the Space Age in a Christmas poem in the *Pulpit* magazine. He wrote:

> Oh, traveler, dost thou see
> The shadow of things to be?
> Nail prints in infant hands,
> The brow, so lately soothed
> By mother's soft caress
> One day to wear the thorned crown,
> The suckling lips
> So soon to taste the gall.
>
> See the future, traveler,
> And kneel!
> Know the wonder of this hour:
> Hush, the symphony of the stars
> Declares—God is not finished.[10]

The cross is central. But what makes it central? It is only central because of its relationship to the resurrection. The resurrection, plus the ascension, shows who Jesus is. This is the underlining of the incarnation. We need to know who he is before we can interpret and appreciate what he has done. Yet it still remains and becomes more evident that his supreme deed is wrought out on the cross. The incarnation and the resurrection are essential to Christian faith, not as unique separate events, but for the emphatic meaning they give the cross.

The Space Age, with a climate of competition, calls for sincere and effective religion—religion that has the elements of involvement and commitment, responsibility, and a constructive, positive

[10] Arthur H. Kolsti, "At Cradleside," the *Pulpit*, December, 1958, p. 24.

note that indicates not only joy but some sense of purpose or direction. Where do we find these in the Christian faith, the faith that wants to be relevant to a new age? "Come, take up the cross, and follow me," said Jesus.[11]

The cross impels a person to be less selfish, and more concerned with his neighbor. The cross forces a Christian outward in compassion. He is not like the French Foreign Legion captain in Albert Camus' story "The Growing Stone," watching a native religious ceremony. A native cook explained the service to the captain. "Unfold your arms, Captain," the cook said. "You are hugging yourself and keeping the saint's spirit from descending!" [12] In relationship to the Sunday question, the cross would call for consideration of the opposite viewpoint by the majority and the minority alike—a little unfolding of the arms, a little more outstretching.

The crucified Savior brings new freedom to those who accept him as a personal Redeemer. What more could a person ask for in the Space Age than freedom, not merely political freedom which is theoretically an impossibility, but rather freedom of the spirit? What would a man give in exchange for the peace and happiness of his soul?

This then is the task of theology: to make this word of the cross understandable—not through any dogmatic theory about the vicarious atonement of Jesus Christ, but as the word that calls him who hears it to accept the cross. To declare that the Crucified Christ is the revelation of God's grace is to ask man whether he is ready to surrender his self-will (which thinks it can live out of its own strength of thinking and doing) in order to find true life through his very surrender. To such readiness the word of the cross promises a freedom which frees man from himself and so enables him to live in freedom from fear and in freedom for responsibility.[13]

Must we say that the resurrection is the only rallying point for joyful, positive, hopeful Christianity? This then is not to say that we need a day of the cross, a Friday of worship instead of Sunday.

[11] Mark 10:21.
[12] Albert Camus, "The Growing Stone," in *Exile and the Kingdom, op. cit.,* p. 191.
[13] Rudolf Bultmann, *Christian Century, loc. cit.*

But it is to say that there are other factors that demand our attention as much as or even more so than the resurrection.

More practical than a Friday or a Sunday worship day, in light of the fact that we already have a two-day weekend with the prospects of still a longer weekend developing, would be a three-day Sabbath. This three-day Sabbath could take in all of the major traditional emphases; namely, the crucifixion, creation, resurrection. The church's concern would be not a cessation from labor and physical rest per se, but rather the realization of all of its worship goals.

A three-day arrangement could be achieved without forced closings by the state. For example, a communion service could be held on a Friday, or on a Thursday evening commemorating the time when Christ broke the bread and said, "This do in remembrance of me." Saturday could be a rest day or a "rest" evening, with some organized rest and preparation, perhaps in terms of retreat or preparation for church work, such as study courses or merely the preparing to teach in Sunday school or a training course at home. The 1959 national congress of the Romanian Orthodox Church in America voted to use each Saturday for the religious education of its children. And Saturday evening could become a night for family worship, as many Christian families observe it now.

The conservative Chinatown Evangel Mission, New York City, has a Saturday-afternoon Bible hour and a three-hour combined Sunday school and church service on Sunday afternoon. This permits its hard-working parish members—laundrymen, waiters, shop operators—to rest (sleep late) on Sunday morning. The Lutheran Church in Denmark is changing its worship services across that country this year from 10:00 A.M. to 10:30 A.M., permitting worshipers to sleep longer before coming to church. A Mennonite and Church of the Brethren project in Chicago's slums did not begin with a Sunday morning service at all, but rather with daily evening fellowship. The idea was to discourage the large numbers of a bustling Sunday school, and to emphasize the quality of faith through total commitment and concentration. Russell Bow, minister of the Woodlawn Methodist Church, Owensboro, Kentucky, found that shifting the only service from 11:00 to 9:00 A.M. increased attendance. After all, he says, "Why worship at eleven if a different hour is more convenient? Is not any other hour just as sacred?" [14]

If automation and the channeling of affluence calls for greater Sunday labor in certain fields of work, as it assuredly has already, then, to include all, the Sunday observance could be a Sunday fellowship breakfast or an evening meal, including a worship service along traditional or entirely new lines. Pliny, in his famous letter to the emperor Trajan in A.D. 104, tells how Christians in his province of Bithynia in Asia Minor held a service early in the morning "on a fixed day before light" (*stato die ante lucem*) and a common meal late in the evening.[15] Such a procedure would be adaptable to the Space Age. Already this pattern is in partial use, Catholics emphasizing early-morning worship, Protestants later worship and evening services. Catholics go to church before breakfast—perhaps there would be an arrangement whereby Protestants could go to church *for* breakfast, and worship. The evening service, which incidentally is the main service for the free churches in Great Britain, Australia, and New Zealand, could be reactivated.

This three-day, instead of a one-day, Lord's day, especially without benefit of closing laws, is fully compatible with the early church of the first four centuries and fully compatible with the spirit of the Space Age. The three-day arrangement recognizes the increase in leisure time, the current church-state dilemma with conflicting Christian-Jewish interests, the rise of new socioeconomic forces. The new American society, according to John Galbraith of Harvard in his best-selling book of 1958, *The Affluent Society*, calls for the accruements of overproduction to be channeled into service goods. A three-day Sabbath—any period of time longer than the traditional one day, enforced or otherwise (a matter which is not the concern of the church)—would provide opportunity to improve the cultural and spiritual life of the individual and therefore the inclination of a society toward charity and public service.

And there it is. The church has a fully constructive, plausible

---

[14] *New Christian Advocate*, August, 1959, p. 29.

[15] William Melmoth, translator, *Pliny Letters*, Vol. 2 (New York: The Macmillan Company, 1915), "To the Emperor Trajan," Book 10, Chap. 96, p. 401.

solution to the problems of Sunday and blue laws in the Space Age, consistent with the best elements of its faith, wholly workable, independent of the state, dynamic, contemporary.

And yet the voice of the church on both the problem and the solution of twentieth century blue-law controversies should be deeper than a mere juggling of days.

VII SUNDAY AND DEEPER LEVELS OF FAITH

When we reconsider the Lord's Day in the Space Age, with a view to relieving the church-state cleavage and making the day adaptable to the new age, it is possible to find recommendations for changing the day. This could be done in many ways, such as observing Friday, the day of the Redeemer, or expanding the Lord's Day to include all of the major emphases of the church; namely, creation (Saturday), redemption (Friday), resurrection (Sunday). This appears reasonably practical, for the weekends are becoming longer and work hours shorter. But is this change or extenuation of the day any different from where we were except for the possibility of alleviating the church-state compromise or satisfying some other important premise of theology, such as paying more attention to the crucifixion? Does it really make any difference, if we are going to observe a day, which day it is, or if we observe a group of days, which days they are? There would still be holy days; and with human nature as it is, the church would still encourage the state to enforce its days.

Does a stronger emphasis on the cross and communication really face the whole question of Sunday in the Space Age? Are there other factors that a theological reconstruction needs to have in mind?

Consider two parables:

I

A Christian couple are at breakfast, Monday morning. As the husband gulps down his coffee, he ponders the front page of the newspaper. His wife is flipping through the pages:

WIFE: They're taking Sunday away from us, George!

HUSBAND: Who's taking what?

WIFE: Sunday, it says here. Dr. Letskeepit from somewhere told a convention in Chicago that unless the churches do something about it the devil's going to get Sunday, too.

HUSBAND: The devil's already got six days—what does he want with a seventh anyway? Heh, heh . . .

WIFE: George, you don't understand.

HUSBAND: Then to the devil with Sunday, too. (*He raises cup of coffee in a toast.*)

WIFE: Oh, George, sometimes you make me so mad I can't see! (*Husband drops a quick kiss on wife's forehead as he catapults out of door.*)

II

Meanwhile two space missionaries, the first to head for Venus, are skidding their space bullet to a stop.

CECIL: Whee! We made it!

HENRY: Let's see, now—our Bible, our manual, the exterminator in case the people here aren't what we think they are, rations for two months . . .

CECIL: Say, Henry, I didn't see the sun go down.

HENRY: No, I didn't either.

CECIL: Let's get out the manual. (*He thumbs the pages.*) Venus . . . calendar . . . ah, here we are. . . .

HENRY: You know, we should have checked into this before we left.

CECIL: Yes, but you can't do everything. (*He pauses intently.*) Now . . . a day on Venus . . . can be as much as thirty earth days!

HENRY: You mean the sun may not go down for thirty days? Horrors! . . . Only a dozen days in a year?

CECIL: That's interesting. . . . Ha, ha . . . our two-months rations are for two days, then, instead of two months. . . . Who would have ever thought of coming 'way out here with only two days of food?

HENRY: Well, you know, we really have more.

CECIL: Yes, of course. But enough of that. Have you the program all planned for the first worship service?

HENRY: Yes, but . . . which day will be Sunday? These people

won't know anything about our earth scheme of things; besides,
how could you divide twelve days into 365? Where should we
begin Sunday and where should we stop?

CECIL (*pondering*): A Sunday one month long . . . we can't have
any of that. It would work us to death!

HENRY: We'll have to give some real thought to that, Cecil. But
first let's see what this place is like. Maybe the people will have
some ideas of their own.

CECIL (*as they open door*): Ooops! I stepped on something.

HENRY: A bug, isn't it?

BUG-LIKE CREATURE: Ya, ya, ya, kee, kee, kee, koh, koh, koh, bok,
bok, bok. GRRRRRRRRRRRRRRRRRRRRR!

NARRATOR: And the two space missionaries are back in their space
bullet, zinging toward earth, with their two-months—or was it
two-days—rations.

What do these two parables mean?

Take the first parable. Note the satire of the husband. The devil
already has six days, why worry about the other? A one-day-out-of-
seven religion does not make sense to him. If he lives specifically for
Christ on the day that is so unlike his weekly routine—truly he
must be living in hell during the week. A distinction of days permits
a classification. If the devil has the other days by the lack of association of Christ and the Spirit with them, then there is not much to
live for and the man in the parable would throw in the seventh also.
A one-day religion is not worth it anyway, and certainly it is not
worth taking seriously. So he laughs.

You and I know people who regard Easter attendance as sufficient to carry them through for the year. They may be right. Or is
it possible that they are wrong, and that the Sunday worshiper who
gets just enough religion to carry him for seven days is wrong too?
Can a day of concentration on religion be expected to carry through
other periods of time without such concentration? Sunday makes
Christianity quantitative, a fixed phenomenon with guaranteed re-
sults, like a hypodermic needle in a doctor's office. The husband in
this parable is questioning the distinction between days, a distinction
which is beginning to wear off because of many factors, such as a
new commercialism, a new capitalism, and so on.

Living in the Space Age, it strikes him as funny when his wife

reminds him of the traditional duties on that day. He could pretend
there is no distinction. When Sunday comes, he could very well be
serious, with no real change of attitude. He could dress up for
church, and be at the same time and same place as he is with his
job each week. But that is the difference. Sunday is not a workday.
It is a definite Sabbath or Lord's day. Life may be hectic on the
other days of the week, but Sunday is an exception. That is what
the husband cannot see—why there should be an exception, when a
pressing new commercialism and automation and a host of other
realities insist that there is no real difference: the sun rises and shines
on both days, a customer is the same on both days, as are the con-
sumer, the product, and so on. He fails to see why there should be
a real difference. And if there is a quantitative difference, he is no
Einstein and fails to link the quantitative with the intangible, in
this case the inner space of the heart, the spiritual, qualitative life.
So he counters with laughter, and has some innocent fun with the
idea. And while his wife is boiling with anger at hearing his sacrilege
concerning the sacred day, he steals away and gives her a concil-
iatory kiss as he leaves.

The classical mystic would say that religious experience must be
preceded by certain exercises in a gradation of stages. The American
Christian mystic would say, "Go to church on Sunday, and you'll
feel better for it." The nonconformist, such as the man in the parable,
knows better. He feels better in the everyday walks of life in asking
God, on the subway or in the office, to guide him with the day's
decisions, and in then rejoicing as God guides him. Perhaps this man
is a misfit. Perhaps he is a little too contrived to illustrate a point.
Nevertheless the point is that there are men like him who are intelligent enough to see that there can be no distinction of days in the
Space Age, that such an attempt is purely extraneous, if not outdated
—or perhaps we should say, to avoid a charge of humanism, that
he is dumb enough; he recognizes his fallen nature and realizes in
faith that he cannot know all there is to know, and humbly confesses
that he simply cannot make the quantitative-qualitative link that
Sunday observance requires.

Now take the second parable.

Enough of a minister's energy is required to plan a Sunday of
preaching and other activities each week. Can you imagine how

difficult it would be for him to plan a service that would span a thirty-day period? If he were a John Wesley or even the indefatigable St. Paul, who could, as we saw, talk from one day to the next, or until midnight, he might possibly survive the filibuster that would be expected of him.

Seriously, what does one do with Sunday on Venus or on any of the other planets? [1] Suppose there are other creatures on Venus. What does one tell them? [2] Or, assuming that citizens of another planet have a calendar of their own and their own plan of salvation, what should an earth man do, even a nonmissionary, who wants to be true to his faith, preferring to keep all of his holy habits? How can he keep Sunday? How can he know when it begins or ends? This question is a real one, creatures or no creatures on other planets, as the United States selects and trains a group of men, all of them active churchmen, for space travel and exploration.

The question raised by the space missionaries has occurred before, and may reoccur without questions posed by space travel. The possibility of calendar changes exist. Auguste Comte in the last century proposed a thirteen-month calendar, with each week beginning on Sunday and a "year-day" or international holiday between December and January. The suggested World Calendar of the United Nations, submitted by India, and originated by the World Calendar Association, would have the year divided into four quarters of ninety-one days each. The first month of each quarter, January, April, July, October, would each have thirty-one days; the other months would have thirty days. Each week would start with Sunday, and every holiday and birthday would fall on the same day each year. Along with India, Russia, France, Egypt, and Uruguay endorsed the World Calendar in a United Nations vote in 1953, with England and the United States voting against it. Sabbath observers

---

[1] Actual travel to Venus is just ahead. On May 6, 1959, the National Aeronautics and Space Administration awarded a $33.5 million contract to Convair Astronautics Division of General Dynamics Corporation, San Diego, to develop a new space rocket, the Vega, that may be fired to Venus in early 1961.

[2] Billy Graham said jokingly in a rally before 67,000 people at Sydney, Australia, in 1959: "We may even hold a crusade on the moon one day. It is something that should not be laughed at." His office in Minneapolis says that Graham "has been extremely cautious in expressing any positive conviction on the matter. His belief is that the Bible is open at this point, neither teaching nor ruling out the possibilities of life on other planets."

are particularly reluctant to accept it, for this arrangement would have a world-end day at the end of the year, an anonymous day designated with a "W." (As we have seen, the Mosaic calendar had an extra day at the end of every seven-week period—also, a thirteenth month was thrown in occasionally to balance the lunar month with the solar year.) In leap year the World Calendar proposes a "Leap Year Day" between June and July. This would amount to one eight-day week each year and two in a leap year; but what Sabbath observers do not realize is that even now for the individual traveler there are six- or eight-day weeks when crossing the International Dateline. (Factors other than religious help to preserve the status quo set by religion and culture. Not the least is the calendar industry in the United States with a $100,000,000 annual business.)

Actually the seven-day week is arbitrary, and not dependent on the solar system as the day and year are. The culture has determined the week, just as there are some three- and four-day weeks in parts of Africa built around the native market schedule. The Space Age with its new mechanization and push toward efficiency could disrupt the agrarian work week and the Gregorian calendar.

Our Space Age parables then leave us with this consideration:

Are there not deeper levels of faith on which we might base a philosophy of worship than on habits that originated in agrarian societies and that have been kept alive over and even beyond the Industrial Revolution and into an era of new leisure time?

Is a distinction of days necessary?

The decision is really individual. One may not agree with Billy Graham, but one respects the way he comes to many of his conclusions. He explained his own Sunday position to a sports reporter on the *Charlotte Observer:* "The Bible teaches that one day was set aside by God . . . for rest and worship . . . and to be different from all other days. Now, you take golf. It would be a sin for me to play golf on Sunday because my Christian conscience tells me it's wrong. But it might not be a sin for you. It's a matter of individual conscience before God. However, anything that comes between us and individual worship of God is wrong. And that would apply to any sports on Sunday—boating, fishing, swimming, etc. You can't legislate morals. They must come from within the heart. The best thing to remember is this: 'Whatsoever you do, do all to the glory of God'!" In selecting a time and place for worship, the place to begin is with the individual, with the individual later making alignments for worship.

Graham goes to the heart of the issue when he talks about doing all to the glory of God. Our Bible exegesis may or may not lead to his affirmation about a day set aside for Christians. The important thing is that Christianity is a total matter.

If one is committed to a Person to live in a total relationship in all matters, including space and time, it is difficult to talk of a distinction of days. Elton Trueblood, addressing six hundred United Church of Canada laymen in the summer of 1958, said that the problem of religion today is not the lack of it "but the fact that it is decayed." The true Christian life is the direct opposite of the popular kind of "Sunday morning religion," he said. This does not exclude Sunday worship, nor does it exclude Monday to Saturday worship with the same emphasis.

"Sunday is Different!" announced four chain stores in Detroit and eastern Michigan as they announced agreement for closing.

But that is the heart of the matter. Sunday is not different. We merely make it so. We ascribe certain sanctions and a status of idolatry to the day that are not warranted from a purely Biblical approach, that are not convincing from a historical approach, and that are apparently irrelevant to the facts of the new age.

Sunday should be derived from Christian experience, and if that experience is epitomized by the cross, as we saw in the last chapter —with emphasis on commitment, sacrifice, and a new life in Christ —then we find it difficult to talk about a special day, one that has been set aside. Says Wingren: "Sunday commemoration of the resurrection does not stand alone. Suffering and death appear in the observance of the 'stations.' Wednesday and Friday were designated as early as the beginning of the second century as the two 'stations' commemorating the betrayal and the crucifixion respectively. The whole week, therefore, is filled with the death and the resurrection of Christ." [3]

There are things we can commemorate, but these are better re-

---

[3] Wingren, *Theology in Conflict*, p. 122.

membered in order to prevent idolatry of a day, on a qualitative, rather than a quantitative, arrangement. When a day is set aside on a weekly or a yearly basis, it becomes objectivized. It evokes our external responses; we look to it. Christmas becomes idolatrous; so does Sunday. Both by their objectivity solicit secularism and commercialism—Christmas, a time of gifts, and Sunday, a time of bargain sales.

Sunday invites caricature. There are special Sundays set aside for themes in addition to that of the Lord's Day. Reformation Sunday at the end of October, Universal Bible Sunday and Student Recognition Sunday in December, Holy Family Sunday in January, Brotherhood, Mother's, Father's, Children's Sundays, a "film Sunday" observed by Australian Roman Catholics, a "traffic safety sabbath" observed throughout Illinois churches on the Sunday before Labor Day—to name a few. One almost feels like the Apostle Paul entering Athens, as one wades through the literature about the various types of Sundays. The intentions of the Athenians were good, but they were missing the point. Although they had an altar to the unknown god, the true god, they were not able to understand what it was all about. And the reason is not hard to see. They were concerned with external things—they wanted to see their gods, just as we like to see ours in our various aids to worship, from icons to Sunday-school pictures. More obviously, we seek to establish rapport between God and man through an objectivization of time. Consider what the writer of Acts said: "Then Paul stood in the midst of Mars' hill, and said, Ye men of Athens, I perceive that in all things ye are too superstitious.

"For as I passed by, and beheld your devotions, I found an altar with this inscription, TO THE UNKNOWN GOD. Whom therefore ye ignorantly worship, him declare I unto you. . . .

"Neither is worshipped with men's hands, as though he needed any thing, seeing he giveth to all life, and breath, and all things." [4]

Our religious calendars reflect our modern superstitions, the passion for objectivizing everything. Can you not just imagine Paul saying, "I observe by your world-communion Sundays, your anti-saloon and temperance Sundays, your days for each member of the

[4] Acts 17:22, 23, 25.

family, your traffic-safety Sundays, that you are too superstitious? How about some of the unknown days, days that cannot have a religious tag, the workday, for instance? Here you will find the God of Jesus Christ who made all things and who is Lord over all."

Would it not be better for the church, in any and all of its commemorations, whether that of the birth of Jesus, his teachings, his death, or his resurrection, to work the ideas in as an integral part of worship? In other words, how about putting themes into our worship, some cohesion, purpose, some commemoration or expression of remembrance of a high light of the faith, rather than doing this externally, saying as we have that such and such a day each week commemorates the resurrection, whereas in the service and in the lives of the congregation this theme is hardly discernible.

God is not a God of Sunday, regardless of what that day commemorates among our attempts to humanize God superstitiously. God is God of the whole week, the month, the year, the whole life, and he is God of more than this, God of all, without external or spatial limitations.

The Hebrews tended to do their objectivizing in time—the Christian whose God entered this life tends to objectivize objects, paying attention to relics, pieces of wood from a cross, the bone of a saint, the handkerchief which Veronica is supposed to have given Jesus. In 1959, 1,800,000 pilgrims went to Trier, Germany, to venerate the glass-encased Holy Tunic, the reputed seamless robe of Christ. Christ, though he was God, was also man, as you and I. So there are romantic attempts to capture the appearance of Jesus just as he might have been, with Western or other characteristics, depending on who is attempting to create the physical appearance. This is the danger of emphasizing the incarnation—we create sentimental, sweet pictures of him. It is also the danger of emphasizing the cross in its literal context, assuming that there is significance in the object itself, without attempting to apprehend the meaning of it. For it mattered not that Christ died on a piece of wood, but that he died, was sacrificed for our sins. Yet Christians with their religion centering in space, have a certain proclivity toward an idolatry in space.

But the Hebrew is hardly less idolatrous within his objectivization of time, which tendency Christians unfortunately assimilate along with their idolatry of space. "Although Jerusalem as a city acquired a sanctity which Jews have never forgotten, the Decalogue bestows holiness not upon a place or a thing but upon a day, the Sabbath of the week, for which there is no astronomical warrant as for the month and the year." [5] The day is intangible, not something made with hands, according to the Jewish rabbis. But is it really intangible? When it is defined, with regulations attached to keeping the day, a way of life imposed, it becomes as tangible as a millstone upon the neck of a person. Jesus himself did not advocate space or time objectivizations. When the woman of Samaria, whom Jesus engaged in conversation by Jacob's well, told Jesus that "our fathers worshipped in this mountain; and ye say, that in Jerusalem is the place where men ought to worship," Jesus set her straight by saying: "Woman, believe me, the hour cometh, when ye shall neither in this mountain, nor yet at Jerusalem, worship the Father. . . . The hour cometh, and now is, when the true worshippers shall worship the Father in spirit and in truth: for the Father seeketh such to worship him. God is a Spirit: and they that worship him must worship him in spirit and in truth." [6] There are no space or time "objects" that are essential for perpetuation and worship.

It is not necessary to do away with Sunday, or rather the Lord's Day, but rather to bring the Lord's Day into all of the other days. The church has this responsibility. In encouraging the observance of a Lord's Week, or rather in leading its members to seek God's presence in all or most of their moments, as far as possible, the church could encourage many observances, many times of holy gatherings throughout the week. As Peter and John went up to the Temple to pray three times a day,[7] so the church could seek to incorporate a prayer-consciousness into the daily routine of its members. This is not the same as a prayer routine, for then a person's life becomes external. Prayer is the voice of the "deep calling unto the deep"; it is a spiritual calling and communication, and does not necessarily move with a clock. A clock can help it; also a clock can destroy it. The work of the church is to establish spiritual com-

[5] Israel Knox, reviewing *Generation of Decision,* by Sol Liptzin (New York: Block Publishing Company, 1958), in *Commentary,* November, 1958, p. 456.
[6] John 4:20, 21, 23, 24.
[7] Acts 3:1.

munication, rebirth of the sinner, so a Christian will have his own short-wave connection with the Almighty through Jesus, his only mediator.

Not only would a life lived according to a Lord's Week seek to become a life of prayer, praying without ceasing,[8] as Paul actually advises, but some of the definite practices often reserved for church could be transferred to weekdays. Here Christians of the twentieth century can learn from the Christians of the first—let Christians gather with their Christian friends for their own daily communion, possibly before breakfast, or at a later hour of the evening. The early church met in homes. There is nothing sacrilegious about remembering Christ's death on Monday, Tuesday, Wednesday, Thursday, Friday, Saturday, Sunday, instead of on each Sunday, as with the Roman Catholics and, among the Protestants, as with the Disciples, or once a month as observed by Baptists and most of the other Protestant churches. Let us remember Christ's death daily by the ordinance he gave us, and his resurrection by the form of communication he has given us,[9] the reality of prayer—not only that of words but also of everyday actions that open communications. Let us not underestimate the power of the living God—and let us not confine it to certain days and certain traditional ceremonies. For when this is done, God is more likely to be on the outside than on the inside of a church.

The Lord's Week is not only an alternative to current problems of the church in the church-state area and the area of liturgical, and church-union discussions (where Communion is a stumbling block), but it is also an answer to two of the big question areas of Christianity—those of evangelism and education.

Evangelism is one of the chief tasks of the church, in addition to, or along with, worship and sacramental and/or remembrance responsibilities. And evangelism is an area of very crucial concern in the United States, where figures for crime and immorality have not kept pace inversely with the increase in church attendance. In 1957 church membership in the United States topped the 100 million mark for the first time; there was an increase of three million mem-

[8] 1 Thessalonians 5:17.
[9] Roman Catholic priests must offer the Mass *every* day of the year except Easter Saturday, and Roman Catholics may attend Mass *every* day.

bers over the previous year. In the same year, the United States
Census Bureau, after ringing 35,000 doorbells, announced that no
fewer than 91.9 per cent of the citizens considered themselves Christians. This same year there was reported a 9.1 per cent increase in
crime, whereas the population increase was only 1.8.

Is it possible that Sunday really works against the church? It
makes a rallying point, but it is also a decoy in life, a deflection that
makes it impossible to get at the whole area of men's needs. "As
more people join and attend the church, we have the paradoxical situation of crime on the increase, and more people being admitted to
mental institutions because of maladjustments," says Robert G. May-
field, executive director of the Methodist General Board of Lay
Activities. "Church members are content to be loud in our proclamations on Sunday morning, but during the week we stand outside the door where it's safe." Meanwhile, two million Americans,
between ten and seventeen, one out of five will have court records
before they are eighteen. From 1949 to 1959, the number of youngsters appearing in courts on charges increased 250 per cent, while
the juvenile population increased 25 per cent.

Is there any correlation between the increase in church attendance and the increase in crime? Is our current religion so ineffective
that the crime rate can climb as the churches increase their influence? Evangelism is a key problem, and the lack of real success
of it is a source of worry to many.

On the international scene, where there is a tremendous stirring
and resurgence of national and historic religions, the church is particularly concerned. Can the church face not only the Communist
but also the widespread Muslim religion of Africa?

Muslims have always been difficult to reach, but one of the
things that makes it exceedingly difficult to reach them is our Sunday
religion. A one-day religion does not seem to them to be an improve-
ment over their seven-day faith. It is at this point that a Muslim
scholar challenges the Christian faith. Says Maulvi Muhammad 'Ali
in his commentary on the Holy Qur'an:

Every nation has a Sabbath, or a so-called day of Divine service set apart
from the ordinary weekdays, but in practice, the whole day is never given
to prayer. In fact, a Muslim, who is allowed to do his ordinary work on
Friday, gives more time to his prayers than the majority of those who

recognize a seventh day as their Sabbath. The idea underlying the Sabbath is, no doubt, a temporary cessation of the material and physical activities, to give place to spiritual exercise and to holding communion with the Divine Being. Islam, on the other hand, requires communion with the Divine Being to be observed throughout the entire week, five times daily. Thus it gives a real chance to its followers for the exercise and development of the spiritual faculties, which in others lie quite dormant. The Islamic division of prayers is much more suited to elevate a man spiritually, affording true spiritual food to the soul than is to be discovered in any other form of worship.[10]

The Muslim idea of mixing prayer and work, of holy attitudes with the most conspicuous of daily activities, has been experimented with by the church, not as a Muslim but as a Biblical idea, recognizing that Jesus asks total involvement in society, as Christians abide in him and he in them. Roman Catholics have tried to encourage mixing religion with work with their recent French worker-priest movement, where priests worked as laborers. Pope John banned this in 1959. In the United States the student-in-industry program in seminaries helps to train the minister to be cognizant of work and labor attitudes and problems, but it does not really aim at penetrating work areas with the Gospel. Some companies have been successful in bringing a religious message into the work area with special Lenten services. But this is done usually with a Sunday-morning attitude that the workers must wear ties that day and worship in a cafeteria or chapel instead of a work or warehouse area.

The Qur'an calls for the Muslim faithful to pray wherever they are at the set times for prayer. Would the giant of Christendom also begin to stir if Christians could be called to devotion as many times during their daily routine? One has to admit that the Muslim faith does have the edge on us at this point, but it does not have to.

Consider the problem of education. It is conceded that a child's education is a total thing; he cannot be taught one way at home and another at school, and expect one way to win out over the other. There needs to be correlation. There needs to be correlation between the church and home, too. And not only do we need to orientate a child's religious education with his whole arena of life,

[10] Maulvi Muhammad 'Ali, *The Holy Qur'an, Arabic Text, Translation and Commentary* (Lahore, Pakistan: Ahmadiyyah Anjuman Isha'at Islam, 1951), p. 1061.

but we need more time with him. The Hebrew Sabbath school, where youngsters learn Hebrew that seminary students have difficulty learning or retaining at a much later age, has been a strong and successful approach for the Jew. The churches have toyed around with released-time education, trying to teach in the schools, then to take school time to teach away from the school premises. Has it ever occurred to parents and ministers that the pupil's day is short enough, that he could attend a church education program every morning before school or after school just as well as he can carry newspapers or watch the early show or play baseball? "It is time that the churches get out of the rut of being solely concerned with a short and pathetically ineffective one hour period of religious instruction on Sundays and find some way to carry on a seven-day program designed to meet the needs of all the people." [11]

We need to get the child exposed to the Christian faith during the week, just as we need to expose the worker, if the future generation is to be any more effective spiritually than the present generation. The first step is to pick up the loose ends and talk of Christianity as a unit. "The lives of growing persons . . . cannot be divided into compartments. A child acts as a complete individual in all his relationships and experiences. He does not learn to know God at one time and learn to get along with his fellow men at another time. Neither is it possible to draw a clear line of distinction between the religious and the secular in a child's life." [12]

The dilemma faced by our youth, and adults as well, is caught in the *Lutheran* magazine, July 9, 1958. "Eloise Goes to Sunday School" is about Evelyn Rudie, who plays Eloise and a host of other roles in the movies and television and who has a weekday schedule that "looks just like that of any other successful movieland star. But on Sunday, Evelyn Rudie becomes Evelyn Bernauer and goes to church with her parents." How many other boys and girls put on their Sunday best on Sunday morning for a day wholly different from their other days?

This one-day religion, H. W. Fox points out, is the heart of the

[11] Statement by the National Christian Council of Japan, January, 1959.
[12] From "Goals for the Christian Education of Children," copyright 1945 by The International Council of Religious Education, now the National Council of Churches, p. 5.

problem in the educational practices of Western religion. He says in his book *The Children's Approach to Religion,* first published in England:

I suppose you and I and most people who have had any Christian teaching have been taught to look upon Sunday as so entirely different from the other days of the week, a day perhaps, of negations when we had to live quite a different kind of life, that we have been in real danger of making a difference between our conduct on Sunday and our conduct on Saturday or Monday. In a certain way, though it may seem absurd, I am not quite sure that we ought to connect Sunday with clean clothes or best clothes or extra good food. There is a danger of this of giving a false meaning to Sunday, for isn't its difference from other days more a difference of opportunity, that is, of degree, than of kind? Our plan of ordered life makes any rearrangement of the week quite impossible, but mightn't it be good if we could reset our arrangements and, say, have our church services every five days or six days or eight days if you prefer, so that they would be held as often on a Monday or a Wednesday as on a Sunday? At any rate, we should then have a chance of breaking the convention that a different standard of conduct is proper to Sundays from that which we allow ourselves, say, on Wednesdays or Thursdays.[13]

For deeper levels of faith, let us begin with the themes of the good news or Gospel, the redemption through the lifeblood of Jesus our Christ with attention to the resurrection and the fact that he still lives; second, let us translate the terms or imperatives of this sacrifice of Jesus on the cross and the fact that he actually lives into terms of total commitment.

The direction to which we all should want to go is the realization of a "religionless Christianity" (to use Dietrich Bonhoeffer's term), a faith that "embraces the whole of life," as opposed to "Sunday religion," as Editor John Lawrence, former press attaché at the British Embassy in Moscow, says in a new quarterly, *Frontier,* launched in January, 1959, by the Christian Frontier Council and the World Dominion Press, London. Or it might be said that it would be desirable to exchange a "principle" Christianity for a "personal" Christianity. Of course, the criticism will be leveled that we are creating or recognizing principles by speaking of "themes," special "facts," "total

[13] H. W. Fox, *The Child's Approach to Religion* (New York: Harper and Brothers, 1945), pp. 9, 10.

commitment." But two points should be remembered: (1) A conclusion, such as the respecting of certain themes, does not receive any
permanence or quality which we have ascribed by definition to principles earlier. Themes such as crucifixion, resurrection, commitment
may give way to other themes in another age. For instance, the incarnation might appear more important to other individuals in this
age. We do not intend to make judgments on others or impose our
views as principles on others; (2) Our criterion for action is derived,
not from a code or commandments, but from interaction with a personality; any ethic we suggest at all is an ethic of involvement, purely
relative, presenting abstractions occasionally if you wish, but not
timeless principles.

Many people, some even in the Lord's Day Alliance, would go
along in spirit with this idea of the church encouraging total involvement. But they have trouble seeing that something has to yield—that
to get rid of an isolated, irremovable spot on the rug, the rug must
either be replaced or the rug must be dyed the color of the spot. Sunday can either be scrapped or retained with the traditional Sunday
theme (resurrection), along with other themes (and not principles
such as the necessity for a rest day), pervading all the days of the
week. But in either alternative what happens to Sunday as a special
day?

Now we might consider what are the deeper levels of *faith* on
which to determine a type of Lord's Day or time for the Space Age.

What is a faith for the Space Age, or rather, a deeper faith for the
Space Age in comparison with historic concepts of faith? The difference between the conclusions of this book and the more staid approaches of the Seventh-day Adventists, the Lord's Day Alliances,
and other groups within and without the church, is a difference in
what we mean by faith, particularly a faith that is effectively relevant
to the challenges and opportunities of a rollicking new age.

Historically, faith has been considered in various perspectives. In
the Greek versions of the early faith, especially the Gnostic heresy,
faith was a process of knowing, of climbing up a ladder. Faith was
gnosis, or in Latin, *notitia*, a knowledge. The Gnostics were dualists
like the early Persians; they believed that there were two realities,
God and evil. Matter was not totally evil, but incapable of being

eternal or divine. God was separated from the creatures of this earth by a series of intermediary beings, of whom Jesus, Jehovah, angels, are examples. The right knowledge brought the individual, who by his true nature was just a "little lower than the angels," up the scale. Knowledge or illumination was the key to salvation. Christian mysticism developed, with its various stages of ascent to the divine, including, in classical mysticism, meditation, contemplation, and union with God (normally considered impossible in this life). Augustine, trained in the simpler form of Gnosticism, Manichaeanism, which held to the literal dualism of God and evil, without the extended array of intermediary beings, broke away from this area of beliefs to give attention to the problem of faith and reason. Faith to Augustine was an intuition, something that both precedes and follows reason. Thus he argued: *Credo, ut intelligam,* "I believe in order that I may know"; not *intelligo, ut credam,* "I know in order that I may believe." This element of trust or a "leap" into the unknown, without proof, became basic to Luther in the Reformation eleven hundred years later.

Aquinas, however, drawing his premises from the Greeks, Aristotle in particular, who permitted the presence of reality or a universal within a definite substance, argued that one must know in order to believe; one must let the object lead to the subjective. *Nihil in intellectu non prius in sensu fuerit,* he said: "Nothing comes into the intellect that was not first in the senses." He also allowed for intuitive knowledge beyond reason. But his emphasis on logical relationships, with the material being the vehicle for the divine and also his emphasis on the authority of the superior knowledge of the church encouraged faith to be thought of in terms of assent—assent to the propositions and dogma of the church, assent to the physical performances of the sacrament. It was against the idea of faith as *fides* or *assensus* that Luther reacted. To Luther faith was trust (*fiducia*).

Recently the author was reminded of the problem of faith and belief or assent by hearing a Protestant minister calling for belief today, emphasizing the need for accepting certain valid tenets of the Christian faith. New books and articles and sermons appear constantly under such titles as *I Believe in God, I Believe in Jesus Christ, I Believe in the Church, I Believe in Immortality,*[14] and so on. I wonder if

[14] Actual titles of new books by Abingdon Press. Other titles: *I Believe; I Believe in Man; I Believe in the Bible; I Believe in the Holy Spirit.*

we are not trying to create an assent to certain ideas, whether they be God, and a certain type of God at that, a church, and a certain type of church, and so on. Could we not put the emphasis more on faith as trust, faith as active, faith as a commitment, faith with a certain degree of uncertainty?

Now the mention of uncertainty with faith might seem contradictory. But is it? The devils in hell, whom James described,[15] were not uncertain about God and Jesus at all—they believed generally. Yet they were in hell. Perhaps we might give some thought to the paradoxical statement, faith is not-believing, rather than the usual parlance that faith is believing.

"Take therefore no thought for the morrow:" said Jesus, "for the morrow shall take thought for the things of itself." [16] Now there is no room for absolute belief here. There is no thought for the morrow. And if I were to reflect on it, in such a statement there would be an element of doubt, for the outcome is not precise. I am enough of a human creature to have some doubts when I cannot see something.

Doubt becomes one of the eyes of faith. It is not a denial of dogma, of principles, of God. But faith, which is always a question, a commitment, a seeking, an asking, petitioning, confessing, is never an affirmation of traditional ideas. It is always new, always creative. It has room for doubt, but it also has room for the dynamic working of God. The fact that God is here as a hero in a play gives one assurance, but never without some legitimate doubt as to the outcome. If there were no room for doubt of some kind, then we would all be predestinarians. The Christian life is not that simple; in fact it is wholly complicated, involved, with its only correlation and meaning in the activity of a living Christ.

When we assent to certain dogmas, certain ways of doing things, we bargain for and receive a measurable amount of security. But security is not faith. Faith is a terrible uneasiness. Christian faith "is the courage and the strength of the believing man, in the loneliness of decision, to take on himself the responsibility for his action. The Christian faith is this courage and this strength because it is trust in God's grace, which called man into life and gives his life a meaning, even though he cannot yet see the meaning. This trust knows no se-

[15] James 2:19.
[16] Matthew 6:34.

curity except the word of grace spoken to man. And the offense of the word of God is that the word of grace is at the same time the word of the cross—that the promise of life is also a demand for readiness to accept death." [17] Faith is the assurance of things hoped for—confidence, trust, even when one is unable to believe or make relevant in life the nonfactual. Where there is doubt, there can be faith, the strongest kind of faith. "Lord, I believe," cried the father of the boy with the terrifying dumb spirit; "help thou mine unbelief." [18]

When Jesus comforted Martha concerning her deceased brother, he told her that "whosoever liveth and believeth in me shall never die." [19] This is what we mean by faith in this chapter and by the deeper levels, if not the deepest levels of faith. Faith is "believing in (or trusting) and living in Christ"—not a general or uncommitted assent of the devils as in James 2:19, but a commitment to a person, or trust in a person. We suggest that faith is an active, complete living relationship—between the Savior and the saved, between the Redeemer and the born-again sinner. The outcome is certain, yet it is not wholly certain, for the curtain has not fallen on the drama. There is suspense. The last act needs to be completed; the actor must make his exit from this world. But as the various acts are going on in the life of a Christian, his faith is a rapport. And Sunday religion in the Space Age, though well intended and rationalized vociferously, is but an unfortunate intrusion of serious, all-involving commitment. In reality, Sunday in the Space Age is a contradiction of terms. "Sunday" and "Space Age" do not go together. A segmentation of days does not make sense amid the unifying forces, such as Communism and revived religions like Mohammedanism, that compete with Christianity to engulf Space-Age man. Is it possible that Sunday is not the bulwark in the Space Age that we like to think it is? Could it be possible that Sunday is an obstacle to faith?

[17] Rudolf Bultmann, *Christian Century, op. cit.,* p. 967.
[18] Mark 9:24.
[19] John 11:26. Greek: *pas ho zon kai pisteuon eis eme* . . . "all who living and believing in me . . ."

INDEX

AFL-CIO, 41, 42, 45, 46
Abyssinia, 79
Act of Uniformity, 79
Activity, 52 ff.
Advanced Research Projects Agency, 1
Affluence, 9, 135
Alaska, 3
American Baptists, 96, 110 ff.
American Jewish Committee, 117
Anapauo, 48, 49
Anglican Church in Singapore, 93
Aquinas, Thomas, 153
Arizona, 5, 117
Arkansas, 3, 5, 15, 24 ff., 97
Athanasius, 79
Augustine, 72, 74, 153
Aulén, Gustaf, 130, 131
Australia, 3, 135, 144
Automation, 46
Automobile, 8

Babylonians, 55, 57 ff.
Baptist Conference on Religious Liberty, 110 ff.
Barth, Karl, 67, 118, 126
Berdyaev, Nicolas, 127
Berkouwer, G. G., 118
Blue Laws, origin of term, 7
Bonhoeffer, Dietrich, 86, 151
Brethren, Church of, 134
British Council of Churches, 107, 108
Buddhists, 57
Bultmann, Rudolf, 67, 101, 126, 133, 155

California, 5, 12, 39, 117
Calvin, John, 67, 68

Camus, Albert, 44, 118, 119, 127, 133
Canada, 3, 28 ff., 36, 93, 97, 99, 124
Cape Canaveral, 1, 2
Capital punishment, 120
Capitalism, 11
Censorship, 115
Charlemagne, 84
Chicago, 13, 134
China, 42, 53, 120
Chinatown Evangel Mission, 134
Christian Churches, International Convention of, 86
Christmas, 78
Chrysostom, 76
Cincinnati, 100, 101
Clement of Alexandria, 74
Codex Bezae, 60
Commitment, 154, 155
Communication, 128
Communists, 53, 102, 110, 128 ff., 155
Compromise, 102 ff.
Connecticut, 7
Constantine, 73, 76 ff., 81 ff., 125
Constitutions of the Holy Apostles, 75, 76
Council of Laodicea, 76
Covenant, New, 125
Creation, 47, 57, 125 ff., 137
Cross, 74, 123, 125 ff.
Crown Kosher Supermarket of Massachusetts, Inc., 3
Cullmann, Oscar, 48
Cyprian, 76

Day of the Lord, 63
Dead Sea Scrolls, 72
Desegregation, 112
Didache, 64, 75